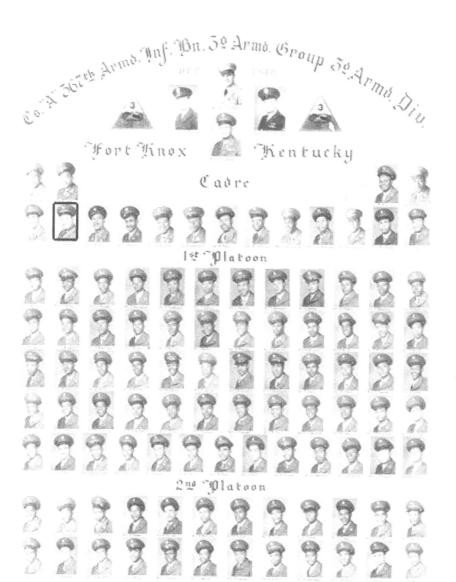

Co. A 367th Armd. Inf. Bn. 3d Armd. Group 3d Armd. Div.

Fort Knox   Kentucky

Cadre

1st Platoon

2nd Platoon

Sgt. Wheeler

A SOLDIER & HIS WIFE'S JOURNEY

By
Pauline Vance Wheeler

Library of Congress Cataloging in Publication Data
Wheeler, Pauline, date 2022.

Manufactured in the United States of America.

This book is dedicated to the Wheeler Family, my late husband's family, and the Vance Family.

FOREWORD

By Eric Pauron Wheeler

Despite the tragedy of losing her daughter recently to ALS, having great challenges with her health, and not being able to sleep well at night, she overcame all of the above and, at age 98, began writing this book and finished it two and a half months prior to her 100th birthday.

This is a true story of two remarkable partners who would rise above overwhelming hindrances and succeed in making remarkable accomplishments during their lifetime. This soldier, Sergeant Shelvie Wheeler, who started out as a high school dropout, was gifted with enough wisdom to heed his mother's advice. He remembered his mother's last words: "Shelvie, find you a wife and settle down." He did indeed find a wife, Pauline Vance. This find would be the key to his success. Yes, he found a very beautiful, brilliant, and devoted wife. A wife who would surrender her desires, goals, and career and become a homemaker or a stay-at-home mom to support his career and rear their five children. Shelvie and Pauline complemented one another very well. Shelvie had great common sense, humor, and military discipline. Pauline was valedictorian of her high school, a star basketball player, and gifted with a champion warrior spirit.

Despite the sacrifices for her beloved soldier, she eventually would rise to great heights through her gifts and have her 'moment in the sun' – winning awards, producing an oratorical CD, writing a song for Virginia, and getting the attention of her local City Council and of course, becoming an author.

Her great source of inspiration was listening to Joyce Meyers, From the Heart Ministries, and Joel Osteen.

What an inspirational story!

Contents

Shelvie's Early Years

This book is a tribute to my late husband, Sgt. Shelvie Wheeler, Sr. Shelvie was born in Triana, Alabama, on June 23, 1913, as Shelby Wheeler. Shelby was the sixth child of Harris and Eliza Wheeler. His twin brother, Shelton, died as an infant. Triana was a country town near Huntsville, Alabama. Shelby's nickname was Boisie.

The nickname was given to him because of the size of his head. It was rumored that he did not walk until he was three years old and only then because someone yelled there was a mad dog in the area. He continued his mischief ways even in the classroom. One day he got in such big trouble with his teacher that she whipped him before the class. I believe that teachers during that day would turn their misbehaving students over in their lap and spank them. In this case, Shelby would later boast about his having the last laugh in that while she was whipping him, he wet on her before the observant class.

As a result of the limited educational opportunities in Triana, Mother Eliza convinced her husband to move to Birmingham, Alabama, because more opportunities afforded their children.

Shelby, who would later change his name to Shelvie, learned early how to save his money and before they moved, he had saved a considerable amount of money and had a few hogs. When Shelvie started school in Birmingham, he skipped several grades to be with students his size. In those days, he said, you didn't have transcripts, and the teachers took your word. Unfortunately, he was never able to catch up. By the time he reached 10th grade, his teacher had become suspicious of his academic level. This suspicion grew out of his inability to correctly use the English language when speaking. One word that was difficult for him to correct was "dis-remembered." Whenever the teacher would ask him a question that he didn't know, his response would be, "I dis-remembered." She soon discovered that he had skipped several grades in order to be with students his size. His teacher knew that was terribly wrong and refused to pass him. After repeating 10th grade a number of times, he quit school and told his mother he just couldn't learn. She told him that if he wasn't going to school, he would have to find a job.

Shelvie began working at a café. He worked as a waiter but soon, his friends told him about the L & N Railroad Station, which was in need of workers and was hiring with better wages. He and his friends applied. It appeared that it was Shelvie's 'gift of the gab' that landed him the job. Unfortunately, not one of his friends was hired.

Shelvie had a unique way of making his listeners laugh in an instant. I can imagine him selling some of his 'lines' to the 'boss'… "One thing about life, it is something like a map. You sit down, and you plan on how you're going to do it, when you are going to do it, and why you're going to do it." I can just hear him tell the guy who hires, "Some people do things and then think how they're going to do it—but you think on how you're going to do it before you do it." His employer ended the interview by responding, "OK, you got so much mouth, come on and let me see what you can do."

Shelvie was hired at the railroad station, cleaning up and oiling the train wheels. While working there, he was drafted into the army.

Shelvie enlisted in the military on April 8, 1942. This enlistment was approximately four months after the attack on Pearl Harbor. He was stationed at Fort McClellan in Anniston, Alabama. His basic training or 'port of debarkation' was done in California. It's been said that when Shelvie's mother learned that he had been placed on orders to go to war, she walked the streets crying as though she would never see her son again. During this time, Shelvie was diagnosed with having flat feet or fallen arches. The medical term is Pes Planus. This is a disability demonstrated in the arches of the feet flattening. It affects your ability to walk or your endurance in walking long distances. Instead of immediately going overseas, he remained in the states for further treatment. His mother would die a short time later of a heart attack.

Shelvie was stationed at Fort McClellan until December 1944. He was transferred to Fort McPherson, located in Atlanta, Georgia, and was there until January 18, 1946. Then he was transferred to a very famous fort named Fort Knox. Fort Knox was named in honor of Henry Knox, the Chief of Artillery in the Revolutionary War. Fort Knox is known to have one of the heaviest guarded vaults on the planet. During World War II, it stored the Declaration of Independence, the U.S. Constitution, and the Bill of Rights to provide maximum protection for those documents. It is the home to about half of the U.S. Gold Reserves. Fort Knox is located approximately 40 miles south of Louisville, Kentucky. Shelvie arrived at Fort Knox, Kentucky, on January 19, 1946.

His Wife's Early Years

I was born in Pendleton, South Carolina on August 15, 1922, the granddaughter of an enslaved person. When I was growing up, everybody was poor in our area. We all wore patches on our clothes. The White children were shoeless, and so were the Black children. The only difference was that we had to walk to school while they rode the bus. I suppose we were about five miles from school and walked to and from school daily and thought nothing of it. We were only anxious to achieve good grades and make our parents proud of us. At that time, the school was called Anderson County Training School on West Queen Street in Pendleton, S.C., which was from 1st thru 11th grade.

The above picture is our school's Faith Cabin Library and also in the picture is the school's basketball team. Miss Madison was our coach. There were no indoor facilities. However, we had fun. The good earth was our flooring. I was a forward and really loved that position. Hattie McGee is holding the ball, and I am standing to the right and the third row behind her. At that time (1941), basketball was played differently than it is today.

This lamp was used especially at night to study our lesson as we didn't have electricity. When we finished our lessons, we would help our mother make quilts as there was no money to buy blankets to keep warm during the winter nights.

Today, the teams play all over the court. My, my, what a joy to watch! Professor B.W. Gallman was our principal for years. He was a great man. He married one of his teachers, Lenora Doll, who was the elementary music teacher. Their union produced one son who became a physician. He was from Newberry, S.C., and Mrs. Gallman was from Hartsville, S.C. They were a lovely couple. As soon as we were home from school, mother had dinner ready for us; then, we dashed out to the fields to work until almost dark.

We got our homework by lamplight or by the light from the fireplace. We did not have electricity. The roosters would start crowing around four or five o'clock early morning daily, and that was time for us to get out of bed. Water had to be brought from the spring so mother would have plenty to cook with while we were in school. We fed the mules and got them ready for Daddy to use while we were in school. The cows had to be milked. We had to churn the milk so mother would have the butter to put in between our biscuits, as that was what we carried to school for our lunch. Everyone brought their lunch as there was no lunch served at school.

My parents would save the ashes from the fireplace to dust the vegetables and the cotton stalks to kill the worms. I don't guess there was fertilizer in those days, or at least we didn't have any. Dad would  set traps to catch rabbits, squirrels, and possums, and we were thrilled over having that for a meal. You could skin rabbits, but Mother would singe a possum in order to remove the hair. Mother would place sweet potatoes around the meat when it was about half-cooked, and that would take away the wild taste. No one thought about the disease animals carried in those days. She used a corrugated washboard at times to get tough spots out of the clothes while we were doing our homework. My father was the owner of 40 acres of land. We grew most of our food.

Of course, we had to purchase a few things. This was slightly different from the sharecropper (as they did not have the needed equipment to farm). They worked for the land owner and had to give back half of what they produced. Economic hardship in the '30s was terrible.

Sometime in the winter, when wood was scarce, she would cook using the fireplace while we bundled in. Mother used an iron pot outside to boil the clothes and a smaller iron pot to cook in.

"A heavy cast iron pot for washing clothes or for big cooking jobs."

This kettle heated water in the fire place, especially when there was no cooking on the wood stove.

This is a goad, grown in the garden and used as a dipper to drink water.

Mother sewed sacks together and stuffed the sacks with straw. It felt comfortable, and we had no problems sleeping. Straw was what was left after the cane had been juiced. The straw was also used to put in the animals' stable for them to sleep on. In the fall of the year, when the cane was ready to be harvested, the cane would be cut off near the ground. We pulled the leaves off and hauled them to the mill. The cane was then grounded into juice until it thickened. It is called syrup or molasses, depending upon the thickness. This was used in baking cakes and cookies instead of sugar. We had vegetable gardens in winter and summer. Our watermelon patch was huge, and so were the cantaloupe and honeydew melon patches. Dad had turkeys, genies, geese, at least two acres of fruit trees, and an orchard with plenty of apples, pears, plums, peaches, and grapes. In the winter, he grew persimmons and locust trees, of which he used the leaves to make beer. He also made wine from grapes. Every Christmas, we looked forward to having a glass of beer. It tasted much better than the beer we have today. I wish now that I had acquired some of his skills.

Pauline's Class Meet George Washington Carver

During the spring of 1941 our class rented a bus and went to Tuskegee, Alabama. This would be an exciting opportunity for us. We were taught about the Tuskegee Institute and it's founder, Booker T. Washington. Now we were getting an opportunity of a lifetime to visit this famous institution. We would also see Dr. George Washington Carver. Booker T. Washington had invited him to come and teach there in late 1800's. Dr. Carver, a famous scientist, whose work with plants greatly benefited and prospered farmers, was still there teaching.

The following is an article about him written by Judy Hull Moore and Laurel Hicks from the book, The History of Our United States, 164-165, (A Beka Book Publication, 2008):

> *"George Washington Carver amazed the world with his accomplishments. It seemed that he was a genius who could do anything with plants. He studied the chemistry of plants very thoroughly and knew what could be done with them. For example, he found 118 uses for the sweet potato. He made flour, starch, paste, vinegar, ink, rubber, chocolate, dyes---all from sweet potatoes! From the peanut he made over 285 products, ncluding milk, butter, cheese, candy, coffee, shaving lotion, lard, soap, shampoo, and ink! One time Carver served a delicious meal to a group of visitors. After the meal, the guest complimented Carver on his cooking. Only then did Carver reveal that all the food in the meal had been made from peanuts!*

We do not remember Carver simply because he stayed in his laboratory and discovered many uses for peanuts and sweet potatoes. He did far more valuable work when he helped poor farmers in the South become prosperous. For years, cotton was practically the only crop planted by Southern farmers. But cotton wears out the soil and makes the soil unable to grow crops. Carver found crops which helped the soil, and he traveled around the South convincing farmers to plant them. He encouraged farmers to plant peanuts, which nourished and enriched the soil instead of wearing it out. He urged farmers to grow soybeans. Today a crop of soybeans is one of the most profitable crops a farmer can grow. Years and years of growing cotton had exhausted the soil and had made Southern farmers poor. George Washington Carver encouraged farmers to plant many different crops and helped the South get on the road back to prosperity."

Our class was thrilled to be part of such a trip! Tuskegee was approximately 250 miles southwest of us. We chartered a Greyhound Bus. Everyone carried their own lunch. This trip would take quite a few hours. We eventually arrived at Tuskegee Institute. We walked around the campus and soon there was a gathering around this short small frame gentleman approximately 170 pounds. Yes, this was Dr. George Washington Carver. What an exciting moment! My goodness! He greeted us but I could tell that he was not very comfortable with a crowd and did not say a lot. Still we knew that he was brilliant and made a great contribution in the field of science and farming.

The Valedictorian: Today vs. Yesterday

I finished high school in 1941 as valedictorian of my class. As the speaker for my class, I had to write my own speech and have it memorized. At least, this is what was required at my school. I am glad that it was a requirement. Being free of reading a speech and expressing it from the heart allows more of an engagement or a connection with your audience. Let me share with you the startling contrast I noticed in the delivery of a recent valedictorian speech that I heard versus what I was required to deliver in my day.

I believe that June is the month when many high schools have their graduation exercises. It is an exciting time when finally, a long chapter is coming to a close. The mind is filled with many thoughts; moving closer to adulthood, becoming independent, and perhaps moving to another area of the country for higher education. The air is filled with graduation stories through various media sources, such as radio, television, newspaper, and the internet. My, my, do I start reflecting. I just know that those students chosen as tops in their classes are excited about their accomplishments and recognition. I also realized that this time of year for the valedictorians who had to speak at their respective graduation ceremonies was a time of anxious anticipation, nerves, and 'butterflies' as they pondered taking the stage after much preparation delivering perhaps a 'once in a lifetime' speech. I say much preparation because, by the time my graduation ceremony arrived, I had already spent a number of months on my speech. Just recently, I said to myself, "Goodness, I would certainly love to listen to a valedictorian speech." It would also be nice to see the graduates with their caps and gowns. I wore a black cap and gown with a white stole. It is always good to hear and read about those who are awarded scholarship offers for their accomplishments. It is encouraging to be rewarded for your hard work. Of course, scholarship offers will greatly help students to pursue their studies at various colleges and universities.

I later shared with my son my desire to listen to a speech given by a valedictorian. He said that there might be some graduations on the internet. A few days later, he told me that there were schools showing their graduation live on the internet and that he would find it on his computer. I was so excited to hear that. I could hardly wait to relive my experience as a present-day student. When the time arrived, the computer was set up and showed a live high school graduation ceremony about to begin. With great eagerness, I waited patiently for the valedictorian to speak. Finally, the moment had come. The valedictorian was being introduced. The student walked to the podium, and of course, I had flashbacks of my day of strutting to an eagerly awaiting audience. When the student arrived at the podium and began reading the speech and then stumbling over words… I was so disappointed! Oh, what a let-down. I could not finish listening to the speech. I got up and walked away.

I am thankful for the teachers who included me in their schedules to ensure that I succeeded in delivering my speech with excellence. Having the speech memorized was a key component of my successful delivery. The teachers coached me and listened to my presentation to make sure that I would not be an embarrassment to my school and my family. I was notified in the 11th grade around the month of November that I was the valedictorian of my class. The 11th grade was the final high school grade for schools for Blacks. In other words, we did not have a 12th grade.

My guidance counselor, who notified me of my achievement, gave me the assignment to get my graduation speech organized. I had to submit my speech to the English Department in January. The English Department made various corrections and returned the speech to me so that I would have January to May to memorize it. It had to be memorized for the night of graduation. My parents were thrilled. My sister, Hattie, and I would go to our spring where the water ran off a rock, and we would fill our buckets with the stream of water for home because we were not fortunate to have a well. It was that place where Hattie helped me with memorizing my speech. The title that I gave my speech was "Climb Though the Mountain Be Rugged."

I came up with that title because life in high school was difficult. We had to use materials handed down from other schools. Some of the materials were deplorable. Some books had covers that were scarred, some had pages missing, and others were written in or abused in a way that was very distracting and sometimes hindered my concentration. Since I had to walk to school, I hated the rainy days because it seemed that the driver of the school bus would deliberately hit the potholes in a way to splatter water and mud on us. Sometimes, I would arrive at school all wet, and the teacher would have me sit close to the 'pot-bellied' stove in order to get dry.

During the night of the graduation ceremony, only the teachers and top students were on the stage. It was a joy to see my parents smile as I delivered my speech. When I completed my speech, I received a standing ovation. Yes, I still have a copy of that speech.

Climb…Though the Mountains Be Rugged

Youth today faces one of the most difficult periods in modern history. With the general economic and social order undergoing a revolution change, we wonder where they will be tomorrow. You enjoy better educational opportunities than the youth of previous years. Youth of the previous generation in the springtime had to help plant the crops, and in the fall, they had to help gather the crops. That is why they only went to school three months out of the year. Teachers only had to be able to read and write to be hired to teach and were paid 10 dollars a month.

Within the last thirty years, the number of teachers in our public schools has more than doubled itself. 'The-log-cabin-one-teacher-school' has disappeared to be replaced with modern structures. High school graduates are no longer teachers but graduates of colleges and universities with several degrees. This in itself shows that education is climbing 'though the mountains be rugged.' Although we have made considerable progress, we still seek better classroom equipment and equal salary for all teachers with the same qualification. The obstacles in our path often look as fierce and impossible as the rocks in these mountain gores, but if we have properly schooled ourselves for the climb, we know that all things are possible for attainment if we are only determined for success. There comes a time in the lives of most men and women when they feel it almost useless to try to keep on against the apparently insurmountable difficulties ahead of them. Mom reflects, "....but they have to tough it out." And yet, they are tempted to give up in despair and stop for all times to come. That's a great mistake... you can't give up. This is one of the greatest and saddest mistakes of life. If life is worth living at all, success is worth climbing for, even though the climbing is over the most rugged rocks that leave the hands and feet mangled and bleeding but... victorious! Meaning that it was worth all of the hardship.

When Mary McCloud Bethume was born to slave parents, she was at the foot of the rugged mountain. She began school at the age of eleven in a one-room structure. She exhibited excellent ability. Not one time did she say, "I cannot climb the mountain," but she continued to mount the cliffs. When she graduated from high school, she was rapidly developing qualities of leadership. Today, Mrs. Bethume is among the outstanding women in the United States. She did not stop at founding a college for her race but went on to Washington, where she established herself there. Her duties in Washington were such that she was forced to resign from the presidency of the Bethume-Cookman College.

Miss Jane E. Hunter, a native of South Carolina, against all odds, has climbed 'though the mountains were rugged.' Miss Hunter is the founder of Phillis Wheatly in Cleveland. She practiced law in Ohio, plus she was a registered nurse. With her book "A Nickle and a Prayer," her life work has been presented to the nation.

Maggie L. Walker was a businesswoman and teacher. She was the first woman to charter a bank and served as its president in the United States.

If success in any undertaking were always easy to reach, there would be nothing to spur a person on to his best efforts; if there were no difficulties to be confronted, life would hold little incentive for any of us, for the harder the way to climb, the more satisfaction there is in persevering to the end, and the richer the glory that seems to shine around the goal we seek. It is a battle-scarred warrior who wears the hero's medal. It is the victor who has fought the hardest and most discouraging fight, which is crowned the greatest laure. It is the traveler who has come to the longest and steepest distance and receives the crown of life. But laying aside all thoughts of reward in the end, it is worthwhile to climb the rocks that are in our pathway for the sake of character development it brings to us. The influence upon our lives of every victory we gain cannot be overestimated.

What we acquire in self-control, persistence, earnestness, and all those sterling qualities that make the true man and woman is worth the effort. It matters not how difficult or how prolong it may be. Character is developed and strengthened through buffering of fate, just as the swimmer develops his muscles by batting against the tide. If we can be sure that we are climbing earnestly and steadfastly, no rock that will be too rugged for us to climb can possibly confront us. Our climbing so far has been easy, and the few rocks we have encountered in the ascent have not been hard to surmount. Well-informed guides have picked out the smoothest places for our feet and have pointed out the heights above so enthusiastically that it has only been a pleasure to seek them. But the time is fast approaching when each of us must step forward alone. The mountains ahead look rough and steep, but we have been schooled to the ascent, like the mountaineer in his climb, and we need not fear to step boldly forward, determined to scale all heights, until we at last stand on the mountain peak of success. Oh, let us climb onward and upward though the rocks be rugged to our feet and harsh to our grasp; let us regard the scars that every hard experience must leave on our lives as badges of scholarship, remembering that God gives his best scholars the hardest lessons and the rougher the journey, the sweeter the success at the end. And when at the summit we are able to look down and see how the very jaggedness of the rocks has been our supreme source of assistance, we can say why we are grateful for every victory we have at last achieved over every difficulty, but we are thankful most of all that the mountains were so rugged.

Oh, pause not then nor falter,

For fate is in your hands.

Climb ever onward, upward

To where your feet would stand;

The mountains are rough and rugged

But victory is sublime.

Step bravely, boldly forward, and climb and climb, and climb.

Class of 1941

A New Journey Begins

I had a scholarship to Friendship College in Rock Hill, S.C. The scholarship was only twenty-five dollars. I had to serve tables three times a day. Handling those heavy dishes wasn't easy. The food was served in heavy bowls at a table, and each person passed it around. Of course, at the time, I didn't know that was my job. The kitchen manager got permission in the second year for me to clean her house and do the laundry. I was happy then because the work was much easier.

I do remember the Pearl Harbor invasion. There was a special assembly called for the Friendship student body, and it was announced that our Country had made a Declaration of War against Japan.

At Friendship, we had a dormitory mother. The dorm mother made sure students attended chapel on Sundays. Basketball for girls in the '40s was different from basketball today, and women were not considered as robust or had the endurance as men. Our court was divided into three sections, and we had to stay in our assigned area. I played the forward position.

After finishing my two-year junior college, I worked in the school system in Belton, South Carolina. The pay was terrible: Just $75.00 per month. Then I decided to go to New York and live with my sister, thinking I could make more money. However, that didn't work out. She lived in the Bronx, and the rats and roaches were just too much, so I entered Allen University in Columbia, S.C.

I believe it was the fall of 1945 when I enrolled at Allen University in Columbia, South Carolina. I only needed to attend college for two more years because I had already completed two years at Friendship College in Rock Hill, South Carolina. I majored in Business Education. I chose Business Education because many of my people were not interested in 'Business' and thought it would improve my chances of making a good living. As far as a place to live, fortunately, I had a friend from my hometown in Pendleton who had already attended Allen. She suggested that I meet the lady that she stayed with while attending the university. My friend called her Mother Swaggart. I located her home and introduced myself. She gladly and so graciously made accommodations for me to live there. During this first year at Allen, I was able to find a job at a hospital right across the street from the university. Getting this job was mainly due to the generosity of a kind gentleman.

As I walked past the hospital, I asked this man who was doing some groundwork on the hospital's property. I said, "Excuse me, Sir, are there any job openings at this hospital?" He said that they were always hiring. I then went inside and submitted an application. A while later, when I passed by the hospital, I saw this gentleman again, and he asked me whether I got the job. I said that I had not been contacted. He asked me my name and then said that he would look into it. A few days later, the hospital contacted me. I was so happy that I was hired. It was a good job and a short walking distance from the school. Whatever assistance the gentleman provided, I greatly appreciated it.

Spring had arrived, and I had pretty much settled into my new environment. One evening, as I walked toward the campus, I heard someone call my name. This startled me because I was new in the area. The sound came from across the street. I knew no one there. As I looked around, behold, it was an old friend. It was a former classmate of mine whose name was Marcellus Wheeler. We had finished the same high school. He had enlisted in the army for a twenty-year career. This tall thin, balding youngster wanted me to meet his best friend. He said, "See that guy sitting in the window."

I looked in the direction he was pointing and saw this 'big barrel' sitting in the window of a building called the USO. I thought, who wants to meet him? In statue, he was five by five. Introductions and greetings were exchanged, and I was on my way. His name was Shelvie Wheeler, but he was not related to Marcellus.

One day, as I was sitting on the porch of my resident at Mother Swaggart, guess who walked up with a big grin on his face? It was Shelvie. Now how did he know where I was staying? I certainly did not tell him where I lived. It must have been Marcellus who informed him. I must admit that while Shelvie was approaching the porch smiling, I noticed that he had pretty teeth. Shelvie was stationed at Fort Jackson just outside of Columbia. He was on a temporary assignment from Fort Knox. The USO, located near Allen, was a social place in the city for the soldiers. Shelvie and I attended some of Allen's social events. Our friendship developed and blossomed into a wonderful romance. He proposed to me at Mother Swaggart's, and I accepted. We proceeded to make plans. Shelvie wanted me to move to Allen's campus, and he agreed to cover that expense. I believe that he wanted me to move because Mother Swaggart also housed three other residents who were men, but they were her relatives. Perhaps, Shelvie was a little uncomfortable with that. Shelvie's temporary duty soon ended, and he returned to Fort Knox in Kentucky. Arrangements were made for me to travel to Kentucky.

We were married in Elizabethtown, just south of Fort Knox, on August 31, 1946. Shelvie's sister, Elnora, lived nearby and hosted a wedding celebration for us. Following our brief honeymoon, I returned to Columbia to begin the fall term at Allen. Shelvie would drive nearly 500 miles to visit me on weekends. I no longer had to work at the hospital. The arrangement Shelvie and I had, afforded me the income I needed to focus on my studies. During this time, the great challenge that I had was how I would break the news to my parents that I was married. Pendleton was a little over 100 miles west of Columbia. Eventually, I mustered enough courage to take the bus home to tell them the news. I was not as concerned about

Mom's reaction as I was about Dad's. When I arrived home, I first shared it with my sister, Hattie. She and I were close, and I knew that I could get some good advice from her. I told her that I was married. She confirmed my fears about how Dad would react. We both thought that our Mom would be understanding, but Dad would be a great hurdle. So I went to Mom first, and she said, "Pauline, you should then have a marriage license. Let me see your marriage license."

I showed her my marriage license, and she replied, "Ok, Yes, I see you are married." My Mother did not complain or say anything negative that I can remember. Then I told Dad. His response was, as Hattie and I predicted, "You did what! You mean you married an old soldier! I thought that you had more sense than that!" Well, I am glad that I survived his rage. It would be years before my Dad accepted Shelvie as a good husband and a good father to his children. He would later apologize for putting Shelvie in the same category as other soldiers.

A little over a year passed, and I finally completed my curriculum requirements for a degree from Allen University. I received my Bachelor of Science in Business Education on May 27, 1948.

I then relocated to Kentucky and lived with Shelvie's sister, Elnora. He would visit me on the weekends when he wasn't on duty. Now that school was behind me and I had some free time, I decided to learn how to drive. Shelvie agreed to teach me. Out of all places, Shelvie took me to a steep hill. I would try three times to get up that hill. The first two times, I would go halfway and roll back down. It was difficult for me to go from the brakes to the accelerator. When I pressed the accelerator, it would take me halfway up the hill, but then I would put on the brakes out of fear. Then before I could press the accelerator, the car would roll back down the hill. Being determined the third time to get all the way up that hill, I pressed that gas pedal and didn't let up until I reached the top of the hill. The good news was that I made it all the way up the hill. The bad news was there was a stop sign at the top of the hill, and

I zoomed right passed it without a hint of stopping. Of course, at that time, Shelvie was hollering, "Stop!... Stop!!... Stop!!!" Yes, I finally stopped. That was the last time he would teach me to drive at that location.

Later that year, Shelvie received a promotion to Sergeant First Class.

Army of the United States

To all who shall see these presents, greeting:

Know ye, that reposing special trust and confidence in the fidelity and abilities of _____ . I do hereby appoint him

ARMY OF THE UNITED STATES, to rank as such from the _____ day of _____ one thousand nine hundred and _____ He is therefore carefully and diligently to discharge the duty of _____ by doing and performing all manner of things thereunto belonging. And I do strictly charge and require all Noncommissioned Officers and Soldiers under his command to be obedient to his orders as _____ And he is to observe and follow such orders and directions from time to time, as he shall receive from his Superior Officers and Noncommissioned Officers set over him, according to the rules and discipline of War.

Given under my hand at _____ this _____ day of _____ in the year of our Lord one thousand nine hundred and _____

WO AGO FORM 58
1 APR 1948
Edition of 1 Feb. 1948 may be used.

Shelvie's father, Harris Wheeler, visited us often, especially during the Kentucky Derby Race. This event was his special vacation time. Shelvie's mother had passed on before I got to meet her. He said that the last message from his mother was: "Get yourself a wife and settle down."

On January 18, 1949, Shelvie transferred to Fort Bragg, North Carolina. The Army carried most of our household things. We put a few things in the car and headed for Fort Bragg, N.C. We had applied to stay on the Post, but there were no available vacancies. We then requested to be placed on a waiting list. We were able to rent an apartment. It was really a part of a duplex. The couple that owned it lived on one side, and we lived on the other side. A few

37

months later, we were contacted by the military that an apartment was available. We probably would have been content to stay at the Duplex, but because the owners were always fighting, Shelvie said, "We need to move." So, we did move.

Soon it was time to have my first child. On the morning of January 23, 1950, I felt the need to have Shelvie take me to the hospital on his way to work because the 'pain' was occurring too frequently. According to the class I took for expectant mothers, the instructor informed us to time the pain. When the pain began occurring with a certain frequency, we were to go to the hospital. Shelvie would call that night, and the nurse informed him that we had a baby boy that looked just like him. Shelvie and his soldier friend came out. He was thrilled to see his son. My Mother from Pendleton, S.C., would soon come to visit. When she arrived by bus, she called. It was nice to have her around for a few days.

When Mother heard that I was going to Germany, I was told she cried like a baby. She would say, "My daughter is going across the sea."

In September 1950, we boarded a plane for a flight from N.C. to Florida. Shelvie was holding Shelvie Jr. as we boarded the plane to make a connection with the ship that was taking us to Germany. The voyage would take seven days and seven nights. It was a horrible experience as I was seasick the whole seven days. As soon as I reached land, I was able to enjoy food again. I missed out on some wonderful meals. One night aboard the ship was a terrible storm, and of all nights, Shelvie was on duty. The storm had us rocking all night long. I felt that we all would drown that night. We were tossed from side to side. So glad the beds were fastened to the wall. Of course, Jr. slept through it all, and I didn't know what direction to look for my husband. What a horrifying experience! And, my goodness, that was the only night my husband had duty.

What a pity. I was frightened beyond words. It was a relief to hear by intercom that we would soon be landing. I was so glad to see the land. A band was greeting us with lovely music as we exited the ship in Bremerhaven, Germany, a port city near the North Sea. The Army sent a bus to take us to where we would stay. We stayed on the base in Frankfurt. Everyone had to use the same kitchen. That is, everyone in the building had to use the same kitchen. Our stay was a short stay in Germany. We were there for around nine months.

We returned to the U.S. in the late spring of 1951, and Shelvie was stationed at Fort Jackson. S.C. Harris was born very shortly after he arrived in the states on June 7, 1951. Shelvie got 'quarters,' and we stayed at Fort Jackson. We soon transferred to Savannah, Georgia's Fort Stewart, and stayed at an apartment in Savannah. Pauron was born in Savannah in August 1952.

Shelvie got orders for another tour in Germany. This time he would travel without his three boys and me. Shelvie took me to Pendleton, S.C., which was about a four-hour drive. This is where my parents lived. Shelvie went on to Fort Jackson to prepare for travel to Germany.

Case of the Forged Money Order

While I was in Pendleton waiting to get travel instructions, I got a letter from Shelvie, who was already stationed in Germany. He was requesting for me to send him some money, and I went to the post office to get a money order, and I sent Shelvie what he had requested. I later got another letter from Shelvie, basically saying, "What's wrong?"

"Why haven't you sent me the money?" My comrades are all telling me, "Jody's got your money!" I was so disappointed in how he accused me in that letter.

I knew that he was hot. Well, I became hot for his lack of trust in me. I sat right down and immediately wrote him a letter in my defense. I wrote, "I don't know what makes you think that way, and I have always come to your rescue. Next, I went to the post office and told the postal clerk what had happened. The clerk said, "I do remember you getting that money order." She asked, "Where did you send it?" I had a letterhead in my pocketbook. I gave it to her, and she went to the back.

She returned with a copy of the money order, an address, and the name of the person in that department. I looked at the money order and could tell it was not my husband's signature. I told the clerk that the signature was not my husband's. The clerk told me to write to the department head and tell him what I had told her. I followed those instructions. I would later get a letter from Shelvie. He explained that the department head had the information he needed to launch a thorough investigation. He had all the employees of the post office that the money order went to come to his office. One by one, he had each employee write Shelvie's name. When the department head recognized the signature that matched the signed money order, he identified the person that forged his name on the money order and then told all the others who had signed that they were dismissed, for he had found the thief. The department head had the thief write Shelvie a letter of apology and write Shelvie a check for the money he stole. Shelvie apologized for the way he had communicated to me. He said, "Forgive me for acting like a child."

Sarge purchased this car while in Germany. He wanted something for himself to get around in. I didn't dare try to learn how to operate it.

During this time, Shelvie and I were attending a ball game, and one of his friends asked him to take care of his wife while he ran an error. Shelvie yelled, "Yes! O, I have two wives now."

This was Pauron's dog while in Germany. Oh, how he loved that dog! This picture shows him outside the apartment playing. When Sarge was sent back to the states, he said that the flight back was too expensive for pets, so he gave Bobby to one of his friends. Oh, that broke Pauron's heart, as he really loved his pet, Bobby.

43

The second trip to Germany was without my husband, and I flew this time with three boys. This trip was a sweet journey because I didn't get sick, which spoiled my first journey. On the second journey, I purchased two leashes, fastened two boys to my side, and held the other in my arms. There was no trouble keeping up with the boys as some mothers had experience with their children. We were in New York about three days before the scheduled flight was ready for boarding. It was a sweet journey.

Erika was born in Heidelberg, Germany. I don't look too happy in this picture, which may be because we had to depart from Germany soon after her birth. She was born in July, and we had to relocate back to the states in September. Preparing Erika, who was just an infant, Pauron was 3, Harris was 4, and Junior was 5, for a trip from Germany to the U.S. was not an easy task, but we made it back in tack and settled in Columbia, S.C.

Erika was the only girl. It was a joy watching her grow. So many times, she would cry when the boys left for school because she wanted to tag along with them. Erika just couldn't understand why she had to wait until she was six years old. She really enjoyed going to see her grandmother and spending time on the farm. I think it was the open space and the animals that fascinated her. After mother passed away, Erika always regretted not spending more weekends with her. She also enjoyed sitting in her grandfather's lap in his favorite rocking chair, and they rocked until both fell asleep.

Dad and his children: From left to right: Harris, Erika, Sarge, Shelvie Jr., and Pauron. He would talk to them often about life's

45

journey. For example, he would say, "Be determined and full of enthusiasm! Enthusiasm is an art which will fill your work with glory and crown it with success if you just practice using it. Disappointments come to everyone. Learn to forget these as quickly as possible. Begin with small issues and gradually build a resistance against larger ones. Hold an error or mistake, or disappointment only long enough to learn a lesson from it. Make a mental note of how you might have combated the situation with a different attitude or action. Then instantly push it out of your mind. All of us must learn how to make the best of unexpected difficulties. The trick to forgetting unpleasantness is to concentrate on the future. When a plan goes wrong, immediately start to think of another one. Don't waste time on what might have been. Enthusiasm begins with the art of forgetting yesterday's sorrow. If you learn to put each hour behind you without dwelling on its bitterness, inter-strength will slowly develop."

Third Court Martial Won with No Attorney

Shelvie was inducted into the military four months after the Pearl Harbor invasion: on April 8, 1942. This was during the World War II era. He was 29 years of age. Because of a medical condition with his foot, he remained stationed in the U.S. It was not until 1950 that he received orders for overseas duty. His service record up until that time was excellent. In January 1949, he received a promotion to SFC (Sergeant First Class) when he was stationed at Fort Knox, Kentucky but was soon transferred to Fort Bragg, North Carolina. The next recommendation for promotion would come in August 1951, just following a tour in Frankfurt, Germany. He received this recommendation for promotion from SFC to M/Sgt. (Master Sergeant) when he was stationed at Fort Jackson, South Carolina. The character rating that was included with that recommendation was "Excellent." His efficiency rating was also rated as "Excellent." His branch of service was "Infantry." The recommendation for promotion was submitted to the Commanding Officer of the 13th Infantry at Fort Jackson, South Carolina.

As my husband would say, "Let's be frank." During Shelvie's era of service, it was tougher times for soldiers of color. Shelvie did not have any apprehension about confronting authority. In other words, Shelvie had 'too much mouth.' I could not get through to him not to have so much to say. Of course, I must say that he was well respected among his fellow soldiers. One time a soldier hit Shelvie, and two other soldiers immediately came to his aid and jumped on this soldier and warned him not to hit their Sergeant. If it was wrong, Shelvie did not keep quiet. As an unwritten rule, he was to abide by the double standard set by society. His pressing against that double standard resulted in the number of court cases he had to endure.

Shelvie's second tour duty was in Knielingen, Germany, between 1952 and 1955. On December 8, 1953, Shelvie was accused of not following instructions by a First Lieutenant. Papers were submitted informing Shelvie of the charges filed against him. The charge was that "without proper authority, (he) failed to go at the time prescribed to his appointed place of duty, to wit: Guard Mount." which was subject to the Uniform Code of Military Justice. Shelvie pleaded 'not guilty,' but the result of the finding was 'guilty.' Shelvie was sentenced to a thirty-day restriction to the battery area.

Later, the action submitted by the Lieutenant was withdrawn and substituted with a lesser offense that reduced his sentence to a fourteen-day restriction to the battery area.

On June the 5th, 1955, around 7:15 p.m., Shelvie was stopped and given a ticket. He was cited for a traffic violation. I remember Shelvie coming home that day and telling me that a German policeman had given him a ticket. He said he could not understand why he was given a ticket.

Eventually, Shelvie would be charged with a traffic violation and giving false information, a violation of Article 107 of the Uniform Code of Military Justice.

His records would later have only one violation, and that is because records are kept of court-martial convictions, but no entries are made in the "Records of Trials by Court Martial" if there is no conviction. Regarding the violation of Article 107, Shelvie pleaded "not guilty" to the charge, but the findings resulted in a "guilty" charge. The initial sentence was "to forfeit $100 per month for four months". Later, by order of the Lieutenant Colonel, Shelvie received a sentence of two months forfeiture of $100.00 per month.

In the case covering the traffic violation, Shelvie said he would not pay a lawyer to handle his case. He had resolved to handle the case himself without a lawyer because he knew he was innocent of the charges. The officer who gave Shelvie a ticket appeared in court during the court hearing. As the court proceedings began regarding Shelvie's traffic violation, Shelvie asked the judge if he could ask the officer that stopped him a question. The judge said yes. He asked the policeman, "Did you read me my rights before you wrote me up." His reply was, "No." The judge then dismissed the case. Despite the ruling in his favor, his superiors were very angry. He was stripped of a stripe, reduced of rank, and they had him shipped to the states at once. The deployment was so abrupt that no provisions were made for our daughter on the flight. She was only three months old. We had to hold her in our arms. Ordinarily, she would have had a bassinet. Shelvie felt some resentment and curiosity from his superior officers about his well-being, such as having a nice car and lending money to his comrades. In fact, he was asked by a superior officer, "How could you have so much money?"(not knowing that he had learned how to save his money at an early age) Shelvie responded, "That's your job to find that out."

We arrived in New York around September 1955. He purchased a car and drove his family to Pendleton, S.C. He got an extraordinary deal on the car. The management admitted that the salesman sold the car too cheap or too far under its value. It was a new car, and Shelvie was making monthly payments. They decided that they were going to track Shelvie down and modify the contract. After arriving in Pendleton, Shelvie got a call from the dealership. Shelvie had to go to a neighbor's house to take the call because my parents did not have a phone. They apparently told Shelvie that they needed to adjust the monthly payments or for him to bring the car back. He told them, "If you want this car, come down and get it, but I'm not going to break the contract." For them to come to get the car, they would have to drive nearly 800 miles. Well, I guess they could have flown down, but apparently, it wasn't worth the trouble because that was the last he heard from them about it.

While Shelvie was on leave from the military or furlough, we stayed with my parents in Pendleton. Shelvie used this time to get his court martial records cleared and his stripe back. He drove to Washington, D.C., and filled out the necessary papers to have those corrections made. One of the forms that he filled out was the "Application for Correction of Military or Naval Record." On that form, Shelvie requested:

"Court Martial taken off my records, my efficiency and character rating corrected and refund all pay from the incidents."

Line 14 of the form said: "I request the following correction of error or unjust in the following particulars." His response:

1. *Relying on "hear say."*

2. *Passing statements from one person to another without testing my ability to determine my efficiency.*

3. *Not giving me ample time to perform in the capacity for which I was reduced*

Line 15 of the form said: "In support of this application, I submit as evidence the following." His response:

1. *The Court Martial Procedure.*

2. *Board's Action.*

3. *Orders pertaining to my 1st and 2nd class gunners examination.*

4. *An order showing that I was put in for promotion to M/sgt.*

5. *Seventh Army Academy diploma.*

6. *Leaders Course Third Army Division diploma.*

7. *A picture is included that was taken during the time that I was working in the capacity of an officer at the Seventh Army Academy. The band on my left arm certifies that I was chosen as a leader in the school. This picture was also taken during an inspection of my platoon.*

Passport
Photo
July 7, 1954

Harris   Junior

Pauron

The following is a copy of Shelvie's letter to the Army Board for Correction.

Address Deleted

The following is the reply from the "Army Board for Correction of Military Records."

DEPARTMENT OF THE ARMY
OFFICE OF THE ASSISTANT SECRETARY
WASHINGTON 25, D. C.

AG 201   WHEELER, Shelvie
         34 167 591

MEMORANDUM FOR THE ADJUTANT GENERAL:

It is requested that the applicant and counsel, if any, be notified that following examination and consideration of the application and records, the Army Board for Correction of Military Records on ____30 DEC 1957____ determined that insufficient evidence has been presented to indicate probable material error or injustice, and the application is denied.

The notice to the applicant will be in the form prescribed by the memorandum from Executive Secretary, Army Board for Correction of Military Records to The Adjutant General, subject, Notice of Denial of Application for Correction of Military Records, dated 10 August 1955.

Signature Deleted

Executive Secretary
Army Board for Correction
of Military Records

Unfortunately, Shelvie was denied correction of his records but was awarded his original rank.

In a short while, he was stationed at Nantucket, Massachusetts. I, along with the kids, lived in Elizabeth, New Jersey. In November of 1957, Shelvie reported to an overseas replacement station at Fort Lewis, Washington, to do his final tour in Korea.

Upon returning to the states in September 1959, he closed out his military career at Fort Jackson, South Carolina.

Reuben Bernard Wheeler was born on January 6, 1960, at Fort Jackson. He would be the 5th child. I was so glad we could settle down with my four sons and daughter. Eventually, we purchased a home in Columbia, South Carolina.

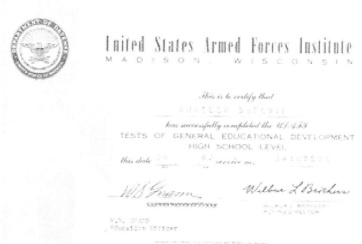

Shelvie Wheeler's High School Diploma

Shelvie successfully completed his GED tests at the U.S. Armed Forces Institute in June 1962. This is the equivalent of high school education. Shelvie collected as many pamphlets as he could find. I would read a portion and give him a quiz at night. We had fun learning what he had missed. Of course, he was already a master in arithmetic, and that's where he made the highest points. My husband was determined to retire from the army. At that time, the segregated army was told if they didn't have a high school education, they were not eligible for retirement. Some had only two or three years before retiring. Oh! They were very disappointed. What a sad time. Also, some were unaware of listing any ailment of any kind on their retirement record, which would increase their monthly check. We were thrilled when it was all over. Sergeant Shelvie Wheeler, Sr., retired on February 1, 1963

Sergeant Wheeler Retires

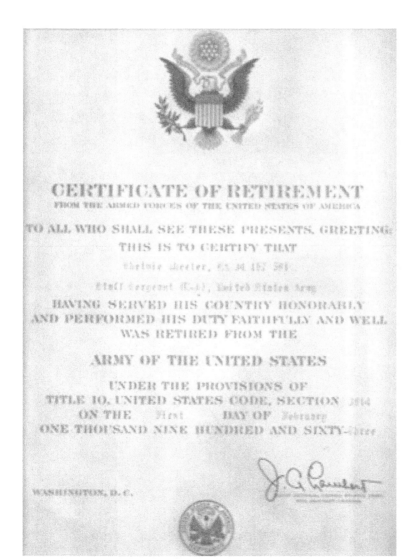

The United States of America
honors the memory of

Shelvie Wheeler

*This certificate is awarded by a grateful
nation in recognition of devoted and
selfless consecration to the service
of our country in the Armed Forces
of the United States.*

President of the United States

Above is the artwork of one of Sgt. Wheeler's men in his platoon. I wish I knew his address to send him a word of thanks. So many of the soldiers, he said, complimented him on the way he trained them.

Sgt. Wheeler retired in Columbia, S.C., after spending 21 years in the army. He was well recognized by students through that rough journey. He operated a grocery store located at 1018 Price Avenue, which was a one-half block from where we lived.

During this time.... It's a scene while attending one of the night-clubs in Columbia, S.C., with Viola Bryant. She loved to dance. Once there was a holiday event at one of the clubs while her husband was overseas. She called and asked me if my husband would carry her to the dance. My answer was yes. I understand they had a great time. After the affair, she sent him home in a cab as he had consumed too many drinks. Shelvie went over the next day to get the car. He was embarrassed, as I had warned him of his drinking habits. I know she and he loved to dance. I understand she was a hired dancer at one of the nightclubs in New York.

Kids First To Integrate School: Front Page News

Weather

Columbia Schools Integrate Quietly

Integration Comes Quietly

The State Newspaper had a front-page article on integration in Columbia, South Carolina. Shelvie escorted two of our sons to Wardlaw Junior High School. This was a special moment in our city's history in 1964. He was instructed by Principle Bristow to have them there about ten minutes after the bell ranged so the school grounds would be cleared of students. News reporters asked him if he was afraid, and his answer was NO. Shelvie said that he was at home among his own people, but when he was overseas, he was afraid. My son, Pauron, pictured to the right of his dad, said, "Dad wasn't afraid because he didn't have to go through the persecution!"

Community Grocery Store

Grocers give away knowledge

Wheelers' store puts
children's minds first

Store

Now that his four children are grown, he's found a couple of dozen to replace them. Being ex-military, he finds his work as patriotic as it is fun. He felt like he was not only an asset to the neighborhood, but spending time with children made South Carolina and the whole Country stronger.

Community Grocery Store is the place that "Sarge" really enjoyed. During the morning hours is when most of the adult women would come in with their problems, and he pretended to be the great problem solver. After a long conversation, they would leave happy. Most of the elderly women felt like movie stars. He loaded them with compliments. It was always a beautiful garment or a becoming hairstyle. Most of the men wanted business advice. Then, some would say, you sure help me keep the children under control. All I have to say is: "I will tell Sarge on you if you don't mind me." He needed no advertisement. His personality did the trick. He was always giving his children advice too. He would say, "I feel like my purpose is to equip and empower our youth with essential knowledge, skills, and resources to facilitate the correct steps to manhood, fatherhood, and of course, I hope, a healthy marriage. Fatherhood brings security to the lives of his children. When fathers spend time with their children, they are reassured of his relating to them on a very personal level. It gives them a chance to become talkative and especially more affectionate. Each child is unique and must be handled differently. A father plays a critical role in his family as well as the community. We are to be head of the household, provide, protect, and give instruction. A wise child heeds their father's instruction. A responsible father is able to give direction and purpose to his children, and in return, they will hold him in high esteem. I tried to lead by example and therefore earned the respect of my community," says Shelvie. "I am proud of that."

Shelvie, Pauline & Rex

Standing by

Shawn Wheeler pickets at Gervais and Main streets in front of the State House as the Legislature meets for an unusual Friday session to discuss education. Wheeler's sign advocates more discipline and no more tax money for schools.

Wheeler decided to practice his right to petition the government for a redress of grievances. He paraded back and forth in front of the Richland County office building at 2020 Hampton for several hours. He held a colorful placard in his hand that complained of the effect of property reassessment. The sign read: With this high tax assessment, will senior citizens make it off their fixed income? Can renters make it off their income? They can't afford the increase. He was the first picketer to show up at the assessor's office building. Thousands of other residential property owners have filed protests and are awaiting appeal hearing

Sarge and His Sayings

I always used to tell my men in basic training,
    If you've been in jail or trouble,
        I don't want to know.
    I don't want to know what you have done.
    I want to know what you are going to do.
        I tell that to my own children.

Don't down the man that is down today
Cheer him in his sorrow
This old world is a funny world
You may be down tomorrow

A loving message to Pauline:

My Love
Your husband

One thing about life; it is something like a map
You sit down and you plan on:
How you're going to do it,
When you're going to do it
Why you're going to do it

It's sad. The harder you work,
the harder people look for you to work

I know not what cause he might take
but as for me
"Give me liberty or give me death!"

She got me and now she she can't get rid of me
What you think about that little gal!

He cut my hair all the time
I met him, I think, in Germany
He was real young
George Outen
He and I were very tight

Mr. Outen was Sarge's barber for years, even after he became
blind. He came over to our home and shaved and cut his hair.
What a blessing!

Often different people see the same thing in different light.
Therefore, I will not feel disrepspected
to those who see the same thing different from me.

I feel better than a millionaire feels
and I don't have a dime.
Ha Ha Ha

I learned after growing up that knowledge is power
No knowledge , no power
The more knowledge you have, the more power you have

Work while you work
Play while you play
This is the way
To be cheerful and gay.
All things you do,
Do them with might
Because things done by half
Are never done right

Honey! Do you remember our first flight
overseas ?

The following lines sum up his outlook on life:

Do all the good you can
By all the means you can,
In all the ways you can,

At all the places you can,
At all the times you can,
To all the people you can

As long as you ever can.

Sarge the Celebrity

A celebrity is born in Columbia

Melvin "Sarge" Wheeler, left, shares a laugh with actor Bill Cobbs during a break in filming.

Joe Bowie checks the lights on a cherry-picker.

The late show

Melvin Wheeler, known as "Sarge" to his neighbors, became something of a celebrity this week. His store, The Community Grocery on Price Avenue in Columbia, was chosen as the setting for the filming of a movie about the elderly. Television crews have been shooting until the early hours of the morning to finish "My Man Bovanus," part of a series on aging that will be shown nationwide on educational television in SCETV, in conjunction with Readisations, a group that produces dramatic short stories about the elderly. Is filming the show. The show will star Theresa Merritt, best known for her role on "That's My Mama," and Bill Cobbs, who has appeared in the movies "Silkwood" and "Trading Places."

John Campbell watches for his car before walking his bicycle down the street.

Sarge and Actor Bill Cobbs enjoying a few few laughing moments

Gifted actors came to Columbia. Of all the places they could have chosen to do a movie, the producers chose our store. They caused more than a stir in Sarge's community. Theresa Merritt, a Tony-award nominee and probably best known for her role on the television show "That's My Mama!" and Bill Cobbs, who appeared in the movies "Silkwood" and "Trading Places," were stars in this T.V. special. The neighborhood children turned out in force to see how a movie was made. Sarge was there too!

Sarge*Columbia Record* September 13, 1985

Sarge Wheeler talks about his neighborhood

ETV production creates a stir on sleepy block

Assistant director Jim McMahan, left, director Chuck Portz and production manager Terry Pound outside store

50th Anniversary

Sgt. Wheeler and his wife celebrated their 50th Wedding Anniversary on August 31, 1996, at the Jefferson Hotel in Richmond, Virginia. It was a joyous occasion sponsored by our daughter, Erika.

A Tribute To Our Parents

You molded us and shaped us.

You gave us God's Word.

You fed us and clothed us.

You spanked us too!

We're so grateful......Yes we are!

For a JOB WELL-DONE!!

We LoveYou!!
Jr. Harris, Darren, Erika, & Reuben

State of South Carolina

House of Representatives

On Motion Of
REPRESENTATIVE JOE E. BROWN
MEMBERS OF THE HOUSE OF REPRESENTATIVES
HONOR AND RECOGNIZE

SERGEANT AND MRS. SHELVIE WHEELER

CONGRATULATING THIS OUTSTANDING COUPLE UPON THE CELEBRATION OF THEIR FIFTIETH WEDDING ANNIVERSARY ON SATURDAY, AUGUST 31, 1996; PARENTS OF FIVE CHILDREN. WE HONOR THEM FOR THE LOVE THEY HAVE SHARED WITH ONE ANOTHER AND THEIR FAMILY THROUGHOUT THE YEARS, AND THEIR MANY CONTRIBUTIONS TO THE COMMUNITY AND TO THE STATE OF SOUTH CAROLINA THROUGHOUT THEIR LIFETIMES. WE COMMEND SERGEANT WHEELER FOR HIS SERVICE IN THE MILITARY, FOR HIS CONTRIBUTIONS TO THE ECONOMY, OWNING AND OPERATING A COMMUNITY STORE FOR THIRTY YEARS; WE COMMEND PAULINE WHEELER, NAMED MOTHER OF THE YEAR, AN OUTSTANDING BASKETBALL PLAYER, DRAMATIST, VALEDICTORIAN, DURING HER SCHOOL YEARS, BOTH GIVING LOVE AND CARE TO OTHERS ON A DAILY BASIS; WE ARE PROUD TO HONOR THEM GIVEN THIS 31ST DAY OF AUGUST, 1996, STATE HOUSE, COLUMBIA, SOUTH CAROLINA

Clerk of the House of Representatives   Speaker of the House of Representatives

Pauline's Moment in the Sun

Richmond City Council

The Voice of the People · Richmond, Virginia

OFFICIAL RECOGNITION

By virtue of the authority vested by The Constitution of the United States of America, Commonwealth of Virginia, Code of Virginia and Richmond City Charter, Richmond City Council, as the governing body of the City of Richmond, does hereby and officially recognize

Pauline Wheeler and Pauron Wheeler

Co-authors of the song

O Virginia

Richmond City Council does hereby recognize, honor and celebrate the work of Pauline Wheeler and Pauron Wheeler for their co-authorship of the song O Virginia, which pays tribute to the history and importance our great state, the Commonwealth of Virginia;

Known as the "Mother of States" and the "Birthplace of a Nation", the Commonwealth of Virginia includes the site chosen in 1607 by the joint stock corporation, Virginia Company of London, which became know as the first permanent English commercial settlement in North America;

The home of Native Americans dating back to around 3,000 BCE, what is now the state of Virginia, includes some of the oldest most significant sites, events and people in the history of the United States of America, which includes the birthplace of eight U. S. Presidents, location of the first Thanksgiving holiday (1609), and the site of the last battle of the American Revolutionary War;

Richmond City Council does therefore recognize Pauline Wheeler and Pauron Wheeler, for their tribute to the history and importance of our state and brings this to the attention of all our citizens.

In witness Whereof, we have hereunto given under our hands and presented this 23rd day of November, two thousand nine, in the two hundred twenty-eighth year of the City of Richmond, in the two hundred thirty-fourth year of the Commonwealth of Virginia and the United States of America.

The Honorable Christopher A. Hilbert
Councilman, Northside 3rd District
Richmond City Council

The Honorable Kathy Graziano
President, Richmond City Council
Councilwoman, Southwest 4th District

The Honorable Cynthia I. Newbille
Councilwoman, East End 7th District
Richmond City Council

Richmond City Council | Richmond City Hall | 900 East Broad Street | Richmond, Virginia 23219, U.S.A.

Verse I

O Virginia, O Virginia,
A rich and beautiful land
We sing the name.
It's a story about her fame
The year was sixteen-o-seven
Jamestown survived, "Thank Heaven"!
But not before
They came ashore
Cape Henry was the door

Verse II

On up the river they came
On that old lazy James
Now they remained
Til' Richmond they claimed
To the First Nation People
We owe our gratitude
So now we stand
From many lands
Joining hand in hand

CHORUS I

Where did it start - these United States?
VIRGINIA!
Who is called the 'Mother of States'?
VIRGINIA!
Who will set the standard for the states?
VIRGINIA!
We'll lift our voice for this is our state.
VIRGINIA! O VIRGINIA!

I felt compelled one early Friday morning before dawn in the summer of 2002 to board a bus in Richmond bound for Chesapeake with one mission in mind... to meet with my son to write Virginia a state song. I said, what better way to inspire, encourage and grant our citizens and leaders a reminder that our history has taught us many lessons of character, courage, and sacrifice? With these virtues, we not only can conquer real challenges but also set standards that will inspire our other states.

I can now breathe a sigh of relief because 'O Virginia' is finally complete. This project lasted seven years. O Virginia transitioned

90

from a cassette tape to a DVD. Hopefully, this work will help to strengthen one's resolve that we are and will continue to be "one nation, under God."

Pauline's Recitations

Mrs. Pauline Vance Wheeler, wife of the late retired Shelvie Wheeler, launches her second DVD. Yes, there is plenty of life after rearing five children and 54 years of marriage. It has been quite an adventure for her.

1. The Gettysburg Address
   by Abraham Lincoln
2. The Creation
   by James W. Johnson
3. Smiles From The Bible
4. Heaven's Grocery Store
   by Adam Kirkhoff
5. The Crucifixion
   by James W. Johnson
6. Message For Newlyweds
7. The Gettysburg Address
   Pauron Wheeler, Piano

Pauline and her late husband moved from Columbia, South Carolina to Richmond in 1998. Pauline has had many years of experience writing recitations and poems for her children when they were in school. She desires to inspire and encourage others with her recitations.

In 2020, I was able to make available recordings of various poems and inspirational writings. I memorized some. Some I read, and I compiled them on a DVD. The above pictures are on the front and back cover of the DVD titled "Pauline's Recitations." Yes, at 99, I still enjoy gardening.

April 20 - 26, 2011   ENTERTAINMENT   The Richmond Voice

Seniors showcase their rhyming talents

Eighty-eight-year-old Pauline Wheeler recently charmed the judges of the Richmond Department of Parks, Recreation and Community Facilities' "Seniors Got Talent" showcase at the department's Westover Community Center. She earned the first place prize in the Spoken Word category for her recitation of the poem, "Heaven's Grocery Store." The poem was relevant to her own life story, since she and her husband, Sgt. Shelvie Wheeler, owned and operated a community grocery store.

Other winners in the competition were Cornelia Walker and Sara Archer, who took second and third place respectively in the Spoken Word category.

Michael Brown won first place in the Vocal-Musical category for his rendition of a gospel piece, while Marjorie Wharton and Rufus Bateman took second and third place respectively in the Vocal-Musical category.

The showcase, which was organized by Lynette Williams, the department's supervisor at the community center, was judged by Linda Jones of the Cooperative Extension Service; Loretta Anderson, a Department of Social Services retiree; LaShawn Cleveland, a department recreation instructor; and Martha Jones-Cruden, a department recreation program specialist.

Photo: Pauline Wheeler (L), winner of Richmond Department of Parks, Recreation and Community Facilities Seniors Got Talent Showcase in the Spoken Word category, is congratulated by Lynette Williams (R), the event's organizer.

I was thrilled to receive first place prize in the 'Spoken Word' category in the Seniors Got Talent Showcase. I used the writings by Adam Kirkhoff titled "Heaven's Grocery Store."

Our Children

The Wheelers from top left to right: Shelvie Jr. Pauline, Harris, Shelvie Sr, Reuben, Erika, and Pauron.

97

Shelvie Junior

Shelvie Wheeler, Jr. was born in Cumberland, North Carolina, on January 23, 1950. Junior, Harris, and Pauron had a wonderful opportunity in California in 1965. Shelvie and I got to watch them play in the Rose Bowl Parade. All three went on to graduate from Columbia High School. Junior got a job working on the weekends doing Janitorial work. He was the pretty boy in the family. Unfortunately, he tried to rely too much on his looks to take shortcuts. There would always be some girl around to spoil him. It caught up with him when he apparently consumed some substance that greatly affected his thinking. Soon he was admitted to Columbia's State Hospital, a mental institution. Fortunately, my other son, Pauron, was working there as a Music Therapist. Junior joined his choir, and soon Junior was granted a discharge. Pauron decided to have him live with him since he was still single. Things went well for a while, but eventually, Junior would turn to his stubborn ways and become hostile. Pauron finally had him stay at another location. It wasn't too long before he was back in the State Hospital. Unfortunately, Junior would stay either in a state-run facility or a halfway house for the rest of his life. He was transferred to a special facility in Yadkinville, North Carolina. He remained there for about ten years. He was then transferred to Grace Care Facility in Ahoskie, N.C. There He remained until 2015. From there, he was transferred to Rucker's Adult Care Facility in N.C. In November 2019, Pauron received a call from a nurse that Junior was not doing too well. She

99

didn't know whether he should remain at his present location or at a facility that could better treat his ailing condition. Pauron and Harris went to visit him and realized that he was in need of more of a hospital setting for his condition. Junior did respond favorably to their presence. The three had one last wonderful time together.

Junior was finally transferred to an excellent facility in Burlington, N.C. It was there at the Alamance Hospice where he received excellent care until he passed on December 14, 2019.

Harris Ronnie Wheeler was born June 7, 1951, at Fort Jackson, S.C. He excelled in the classroom and made excellent grades most of the time. At age ten, he started taking piano lessons. He excelled in piano lessons and was featured on a radio show playing "Gypsy Rondo." To master that song required many hours of concentrated practice, and he had to play the song from memory.

On Sunday afternoons, a group of missionaries from Columbia Bible College would conduct Bible study at various homes. Around the age of 12, he spent a week at Bethel Bible Camp and had a blast. There he was introduced to a variety of sports, including archery, softball, and ping pong. He was also introduced to the trumpet. Now he loves that trumpet. After finishing high school, he enlisted in the army. Upon receiving an honorable discharge, he worked as a recreation specialist at Fort Jackson. Next, he became a representative with the Travelers Insurance Company and relocated to Richmond, Virginia. Before that, he attended the University of South Carolina and graduated with a degree in Interdisciplinary Studies with an emphasis in Music Education. He was in the horticulture industry as a business owner and employee of the City of Richmond and Richmond Public School as a horticulture instructor at the Richmond Technical Center. Now he is operating a landscaping and lawn service.

Eric Pauron Wheeler was born in Savannah, Georgia, on August

Pauron is standing next to Arthur Rubinstein, a world renowned pianist, who is backstage at the Columbia Township Auditorium where he performed in 1970.

14, 1952. He began his musical studies in Columbia, S.C., and credits his formative growth and training to Mildred Strider, a former music teacher at Allen University in Columbia, S.C. Pauron also studied under Margaret Thornton, a former choral director and teacher, and Yarbrough and Cowan, a duo-pianist team and former professors at the University of Montevallo in Montevallo, Alabama.

Pauron's list of successes started at around age fourteen when he began playing the piano for Bethel A.M.E. Church's Sunday School. At the age of seventeen, he won a scholarship to Brevard Music Camp to study piano and saxophone. Pauron received numerous honors as an undergraduate at the University of Montevallo. In his freshman year, he was an alternate winner in the Alabama Music Teachers Association Annual Student Competition. In 1973, Pauron was chosen to appear as a guest soloist with the U.S. Navy Band in Washington, D.C. In this concert, he performed a Franz Liszt composition, the

Concerto No. 1 in Eb for piano. In 1982 he became a Registered Piano Technician with the Piano Technician Guild.

In 2014 Pauron released his first CD. Pauron recalls that there were a number of years of disappointing moments as he struggled to play by ear or from the heart as he was classically trained. Now he is thankful that he has attained a level of freedom at the piano to express praise to his heavenly Father.

Erika Eliza Wheeler was born at the US Army Hospital in Heidelberg, Germany on July 9, 1955. She finished Columbia High School and was crowned Miss Columbia High in 1973. She attended Columbia College and majored in Vocal Performance and Theatre. She furthered her education at the University of Michigan completing her Masters of Music Degree in 1977. She won a bid to participate in the "American Youth Concert" program in Princeton, New Jersey, which toured Europe, and she spent two summers at the Brevard Music Camp in Brevard, North Carolina. In addition to "Who's Who" among students in American universities and colleges, Erika continued her musical pursuits post-graduation and in 1982 she was on tour with the National Opera Company. From 1993 to 1996 Erika was a soloist at Second Presbyterian Church. She later became the Richmond Symphony's Outreach Coordinator: tripling the size of their 'In Harmony' choir and successfully organized several community concerts in just two years. Erika was also very engaged in her community and served as the President of the Edgehill Civic Association for several years.

During this time....We attended a graduating ceremony at Columbia College where our daughter was attending.

Erika is standing on the steps, entering King's Chapel A. M.E. church in Pendleton, S. C.

Erika is having fun riding her grandfather's mule. Her brother Harris is standing by in case there is an accident. She enjoyed being around her grandfather and seeing how strong that mule was to be pulling that wagon and all its contents and how big his face was. She was told her grandfather fell asleep while coming back from the farm. The mule brought him safely home. There was only one traffic light in that town, most of the people knew my dad and would stop so the mule could cross and the mule stopped as soon as he got home. Amazing!

Columbia Hi-Life

VOLUME XLIV   COLUMBIA HIGH SCHOOL   ISSUE NO. 1

Erika Wheeler Crowned Miss Columbian

MISS COLUMBIAN

Erika Wheeler shows her best smile as well as her pretty flowers after being named Miss Columbian of 1978.

Reuben Bernard Wheeler was born at Fort Jackson, South Carolina, on January 6, 1960. Reuben was an unusual child, always anxious to help with chores. I remember him reading the directions on how to operate my new washing machine. When laundry time came, he showed me each step in detail. I was amazed. For an eight-year-old, that was remarkable. He was anxious to earn excellent grades and looked forward to bringing home a perfect attendance certificate at the close of the school year. He missed the school bus once and paid the taxicab from his own savings to carry him to school.

At age nine, he started to complain of having severe headaches, and later his knees became painful. The doctors restricted his physical activities. Even sent a notice to that effect to his physical education teacher. After school, he was to have complete bed rest. During his next appointment, a different doctor performed the examination. That is customary for a military hospital. This doctor came to the waiting room and informed me that a series of tests had to be taken, and he was not pleased with the results. While further tests were made, he suggested that I go shopping or enjoy the fresh air. Reuben would be around for approximately two hours. I adhered to his suggestion. When I returned to the waiting room, the doctor called me into his office and stated that he was not sure of Reuben's problem but was sending him to another hospital. The following day the doctors called me while Reuben was on the operating table waiting for a brain scan. After that test, I still was not told the seriousness of his illness. The doctors requested an appointment at Walter Reed Hospital in Washington, D.C., for further tests. During the early part of June, we prepared for the flight. Two weeks later, Reuben and his father helicoptered to the airport, which was about thirty miles away. While airborne, his father said Reuben's conversation focused on his dad's thoughtfulness in planning for his children's hospitalization so that it would not be a financial burden on the family. Praised his father for being so kind and revealed how much he dearly loved him. When they deplaned, he was almost in tears. At that point, he believed Reuben felt the seriousness of his illness. The following day the doctors called me while Reuben was on the operating table seeking permission to remove the brain tumor. Someone had informed the doctors that his father had departed for home, but they were mistaken. Gee! My heart carved a new cavity. I thought that was his purpose for accompanying Reuben in order to be close by for assistance. Now on my hands was a lost husband and being notified for the first time that my son had a brain tumor and was on the operating table some four hundred miles away. (I was a nervous wreck) I gave them permission to use their judgment. Later I learned they closed the incision after realizing it would be instant death if they did remove the tumor. He remained there for a series of radiation treatments, which lasted until the middle of August. Later, he was flown to Moncrief Hospital at Fort Jackson, S.C. We met him there and were one big happy family again. He looked wonderful, and we believed the treatment was shrinking the tumor. As soon as September came, he was extremely happy. A few children would grab his wig and toss it around on the school bus. That really hurt him. He insisted on wearing a cap and leaving the hairpiece home. I explained to the teachers what had happened and asked their permission for him to wear the cap during class. It was granted.

His scheduled check-up at Walter Reed was during the holidays to avoid school absenteeism. This lasted two years. Finally, in June of 1973, he returned to Walter Reed, which was his last journey there. He came home in August as a bedridden patient. The doctors said that it was just a matter of time. He had been an avid Sunday school scholar and loved music and baseball. When 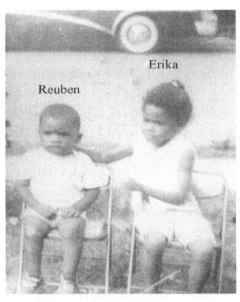 his playmates visited him, he insisted that they attend Sunday school, and once, he asked them around his bedside to have a prayer. That was the flint that ignited my heart. A few days later, he infiltrated another world; in fact, it was September 7, 1973, and he moved in to stay forever.

All of a sudden, there were no children around. No one to prepare breakfast for, to see off to school, to give advice, just an empty house. My husband did not want to talk about him or see pictures around. I was just the opposite. I constantly dreamed of him until something said, "Detach yourself from worry. Concentrate on carrying out Reuben's dreams. Try taking daily walks so the blood will propel through those partially clogged veins. Simply float in the air, and it will equal the beginning of a perfect day."

Life has become a continuous growing flower since I dropped that burden of worry. There is no time to wither anymore, not even under the frigid winter temperature. I have been wrapped in a special oil, like the lilies and tulips. Turn a death ear to the cold season of disappointment and just bloom anyway. There is never a dull moment. I had too many tasks to perform. Joy flows into my heart, the same joy today, tomorrow, and I hope forever. I am so thankful. I found a turning point. Divine arms that protected 0 Reuben for thirteen years are wrapped around me. He accomplished more in that span of time than most senior citizens. His impact on my life cannot be held down. I am better off caring about his ambitions. I have resolved to be an instrument of his life; no more despairing.

Below is a letter Reuben wrote to one of his friends at age 12.

9 August 72
        To Bob Bughman
To my dear friend:
I hope you feel much
better, and I hope you
have a great time
at home.
A verse for you and your
family

The Comforter which
is the Holy Ghost whom
the Father will send in
my name, He will teach
you all things and bring
all things to your
rememberance, Whatsoever
I have said unto you
St. John 14:26
        Your friend

Reuben Wheeler
2220 Clark St.
Columbia S.C.
        29201

Harmful Radiation In Our Phones & Computers

According To Article By My Late ALS Daughter, Erika Wheeler

Erika began experiencing symptoms of ALS around 2010. In 2013, Erika was diagnosed with ALS (amyotrophic lateral sclerosis) aka Lou Gehrigs Disease. To help others, she founded ALS LIFELINE as a subsidiary of Musicians Beyond Measure, with a goal of sharing information and options for those in the early stages of the degenerative nerve disease. Erika departed this life on November 4, 2018 but not before warning the public of the harmful radiation in phones and computers. I watched my daughter labor in research, in study, in experiments, in travel and in prayer to understand this battle that she was determine to win. I am thankful that Erika got an opportunity to share with her fellow citizens what she found. I am also grateful to the staff at "https://healingals.org/20017/12" for giving Erika a platform for the following article:

EMF Radiation: Does it Accelerate ALS?

–By Erika Wheeler, diagnosed ALS 2013

Posted Online by Healing ALS Team December 31, 2017

I have learned thru my own research that I have entered into a stage of electromagnetic hypersensitivity (EHS) where I am very sensitive to EMF (Electromagnetic Fields) radiation. My question became whether my present condition of ALS was induced by EMF exposure. I honestly know that it has. So, as you read the following, my prayer is that you will be convinced that EMFs are affecting us all in a negative, biological way, to the point where you will do your own research and become an active voice in a sleeping generation where many of us are living in a sea of radiation.

There are two basic forms of radiation: Ionizing radiation, in which x-rays and atomic bombs are examples. Non-ionizing radiation is the kind of radiation emitted thru tech devices, e.g., cell phones, wi-fi, etc. The latter, non-ionizing, is my greatest concern as it affects not only PALS (People with ALS) but all illnesses, including those who are presently in good health. An even greater concern is who is protecting us from the  level of exposure to which we are surrounded by 24 hours a day. The FCC (Federal Communications Commission) has not updated its standards since 1996 or 1998, depending upon which source you are reading.

Thermographic Image of the head with no exposure to harmful cell phone radiation.

Thermographic Image of the head after a 15-minute phone call. Yellow and red areas indicate thermal (heating) effects that can cause negative health effects.

For those of you, like myself, who haven't a clue what even EMF stands for or what it is, here is a brief description: *EMF (electro-magnetic frequencies or fields) is ionizing type radiation.* It is invisible and odorless and cannot be readily detected like cigarette smoke or gas from your gas lines. EMFs are emitted thru cell phones, wi-fi, tablets, laptops, and smart meters, to mention a few. There are two types of EMFs: Radiofrequency (R.F.) and extremely low frequency (ELF). On the surface, R.F.s and ELFs appear non-invasive when it comes to health-related concerns, which may have been true 30-40 years ago. But today, our environment has increasingly become well saturated with EMF radiation, rising exponentially, with stronger signals nestled in an avalanche of newer and upgraded devices.

I recall many years ago when a tech would walk up to our homes and manually read our electric, gas, and water meters. Our meters are now being swiftly replaced by 'smart meters' that emit an alarming level of radiation. I called my electric utility company, where I was informed that my neighborhood is slated for installation this Spring 2018. I have requested that mine not be installed.

The data emitted, according to some reports, emits up to thousands of signals a day, where each pulse could last anywhere from minutes up to hours per day. Then add that to power lines, all your in-home technical devices, electricity running thru your homes, and appliances that all emit EMFs.

Additional concerns are expressed in this documentary posted by Dr. Mercola. The entire video is a must-see, for it reveals other alarming issues surrounding smart meters. You can fast forward to 40:00, where the discussion focuses on severe health issues surrounding the smart meter. *https://articles.mercola.com/sites/articles/*

archive/2017/08/05/smart-meter-dangers.aspx Hopefully, this reading will cause you to examine your homes, your schools, your offices and research your own findings and take the necessary action to protect yourselves.

On this New Year's Eve, as I type, my laptop has a protective covering; I'm using a wired keyboard and mouse; I am covered with protective layers of fabrics, including specialized gloves, and I am grounded with wiring running to the outside thru my window to a grounding peg. I am typing in a 4'x 6' area in my home where the R.F.s meter readings are registering safe. You may say to yourself, that's extreme! Not when you are trying to save your life.

An individual once said to me, "I'm going to pray for a miracle that you will be healed." I said, "that's nice, but my joy would be that I recover in such a way that I can share with other PALS (People with ALS) the protocol that led me to that victory." You see, I believe we are fearfully and wonderfully made. Our bodies are designed to heal on their own once the obstacles are removed (including disbelief), and we replenish what is lacking. How many times have we cut our finger, and before our very eyes, in a matter of a few days… it heals! We have no lingering thoughts during those few days of "I wonder if it will heal," for we go about our daily lives, and soon the wound heals.

Our bodies are incredibly made, and because the solution to this illness isn't so apparent as a finger cut, I believe it carries the same principle. We must believe and remove anything hindering its recovery, whether it's GERD, toxins, stress, etc., and then apply a 'balm' whether it's supplements, meditation, organic eating, relaxation, ozone therapy, oxygen therapy, etc.

I was diagnosed, out of town, with ALS nearly five years ago, with the onset of symptoms well before then. According to many PALS, including myself, the same mantra is bestowed by our neurologist: 'There is no hope, but here is a prescription of Rilutek' available to you. I accepted neither. There were no tears. I just smiled. I finally knew what I was facing. I felt I had been prepared for a moment such as this, for in years prior, I had avoided a repeat surgery by applying the same principle. My symptoms went away, never to return again.

One day a few months ago, I was traveling from one area of my home to another by scooter when suddenly my head bowed down without explanation. My chin was down to my chest, and it was as if a hand was on the back of my head, pressing it downwardly. With all my might, I couldn't lift it up. I was frightened, but at the same time, trying to assess the situation. I thought, Oh God, is this yet another ALS interval of decline? In my experience thus far, there is a warning before a muscle weakens. There are preludes of fasciculations, cramping, and soreness, but not this time. I had not yet experienced fasciculations, cramping, or soreness around my shoulder, neck, or upper back.

I continued traveling toward the hallway. Upon entering, my head miraculously lifted up with ease into its normal position. A relief

came over me, but I was still puzzled over what had just happened. Through my research, I was already suspicious of the amount of radiation being emitted from my modems/routers. Upon this encounter, I immediately purchased an R.F. radiation meter, which revealed that the hallway area (that released my locked head position) and another small area (4' x 6') were the only safe zones in my home. All other areas signaled yellow or red. The R.F. meter has green, yellow, and red light signals as traffic lights, where yellow is cautious and red is high alert (stop!).

Around that same time, I was captivated by yet another observation while typing on my laptop. I noticed a pull and a heaviness in my left arm, similar to the previous incident, and a weakness to the point where I immediately closed down the laptop. I had always felt a tingling/prickly sensation while typing, but not where the arm and finger (pinky) became disabled momentarily. This left arm had already shown signs of gradual weakness. I hard-wired (Ethernet) my computer thinking this would eliminate all wi-fi R.F. activity. No, it didn't. According to my R.F. meter, there was an additional red zone signal emitting exactly every 60 seconds, letting me know there was a strong signal of radiation. I remembered reading about

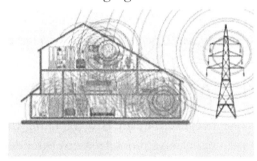

an individual who discovered a second wi-fi signal in his laptop and had a hard time convincing the company from which he purchased it that it existed. I called the company where I purchased my laptop and shared my dilemma. They sent a well-informed tech to my home, where he went behind the scenes (instead of thru Microsoft Windows) and removed the signal thru bios.

We have two modems in our house located on the opposite ends of the house. In spite of disconnecting the wi-fi by way of a phone call to my internet provider, the modem still gave a red alert signal. I later found out these modems are being constantly upgraded with stronger and stronger signals (more R.F.s), and modems are replaced in our homes whenever the cable company (in my case) has an opportunity. I tried purchasing an older model from them, but they are no longer available, which causes me to ask myself, are

we creating a situation of no return where low radiation modems will not be available?

R.F. meter readings were checked throughout my home, including the attic, which registered 'yellow' for caution. We were quite puzzled, for I thought I was only facing modem and computer issues. The meter was then taken outside for reading. I was floored. The reading was still at the same level. Whether it was being generated by smart meters, power lines, or the wi-fi black boxes that are now strategically being installed by cable providers on telephone polls to emit an even stronger signal, I don't know. My brother took the meter to his home, which is out in the county, and he found it refreshing to see only 'green' registering outside of his home. Inside, however, only his modems registered the same as mine with a red alert. The rest of his home registered 'green.'

As I was researching, it was recommended to get a pair of grounding gloves to use while typing, which I am now simply enjoying 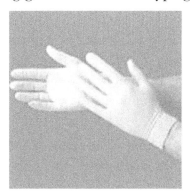 because they are truly blocking the radiation coming from my extended keyboard. I can feel the difference. They are comfortable, tight fitting, and does not interfere with my typing proficiency as I thought they might. Even though the verdict is still out as to what degree grounding is beneficial to PALS, I like the soothing effect it generates thru me over a period of time, and thus I deem it as a 'balm.' I believe the two documentaries, "Grounded" and "Free to Heal", are beautifully and professionally made documentaries that should be viewed by everyone and available at every school, in every library, and every home.

For my cell phone, I purchased a "SafeSleeve" from Amazon, which has a good rating thru Consumer Guide, but I still feel quite a bit of radiation emitting from it.

The R.F. meter, window, and computer shields were purchased from lessemf.com. We were not successful in lowering the R.F. meter readings with the window shielding. I am learning unless you are able to seal every possible entrance, including upper and lower levels, crawl spaces, or any opening for that matter, it's an almost impossible task. I did use some of the window shieldings to cover my computer monitors, and it was very effective.

The R.F. meter can be seen demonstrated by Ce Ce Doucette, a leading spokesperson on protecting and alerting us on the dangers of wi-fi. In the video, you will see her using the same R.F. meter (Acoustimeter) I purchased. I encourage all to view all of her videos on YouTube. For she is well informed, well articulated, and a true activist.

As you see, I'm very much in the infant stage of trying to mitigate the exposure I am experiencing. I have many unanswered questions. If it accelerates the decline of ALS, then to what extent is it having on the most fragile of our society, the unborn fetus where unsuspected mothers to be often rest their laptops or cell phones nearby within inches of their precious cargo; or no sooner they are out of the wound are enveloped with wireless devices including baby monitors?

Back in 2003, Pub Med published the effect of EMFs on ALS, stating there is a need for research. https://www.ncbi.nlm.nih.gov/pubmed/12541277

In the past 15 years, how much research has there been? I'm still searching with disappointment.

Another respected source in the National Library of Medicine cites a 2012 report that suggests EMFs were significantly associated with increased risk of ALS in pooled studies and case-control studies. https://www.ncbi.nlm.nih.gov/pmc/articles/PMC3506624/

My ALS journey has been one of awe in discovering that there is so much information that has been documented that could truly help us, but it's up to us, PALS and small ALS organizations, to find it on our own. Then there are obstacles that scream to be researched but are not. According to Dr. Bedlack of Duke University, our leading ALS physician/researcher, has uncovered at least 34 reversals, and Health Advocates Worldwide has an upcoming book on ALS reversals with little funding. Here are some more interesting points found in the book: "Radiation Nation" by Daniel and Ryan DeBaun, which I highly recommend:

- A mountain of research reports has revealed the effects of EMFs on laboratory animals where brain activity is clearly altered. Isn't this a direct correlation to ALS, where the hallmark of this illness is a neurological decline?

- When sperm are exposed to radiation for one hour, 25% of the sperm count is left immobile. How often do you see men resting their laptops on their laps or carrying their cell phones in their pockets? If it injures the sperm count, to what degree is it affecting the ovaries? If a pregnant woman holds her laptop in her lap, to what degree is it having on the fragile unborn? –

- Wi-fi has been banned at Lakehead University in Canada. The French National Assembly has banned wi-fi at all children's facilities that cater to three-year-olds and under. The Elementary Teachers Federation of Ontario, representing 76,000 teachers, has requested a cease of all wireless devices.

"One PALS used Memon technology to reduce EMFs in his home and office and felt it made a significant difference." U.S.: https://www.emf-harmony.com/ E.U.: www.memon.eu/en/

Dr. Mercola is also a wonderful resource for just about anything health-wise: https://articles.mercola.com/sites/articles/archive/2017/09/24/electronic-devices-emf-dangers.aspx

Knowledge is powerful. Collectively, we are powerful. Please feel free to communicate and share your findings, ultimately finding our way closer and closer to healing ALS.

Thank you, Erika! We Miss You!

From Mom

Shelvie's Parents And The Wheeler Family

Harris & Eliza Wheeler

Harris and Eliza Wheeler were both born in the late 1800s. Harris was born in Triana, Alabama January 6, 1879. His father's name was Felix McCauley, and his Mother's name was Parthenia. Eliza was born in 1875. Her mother, Fannie Slaughter, was born in 1860 and was listed as divorced by the census report. Eliza Slaughter Wheeler was a Native American who gave birth to 10 children. Harris and Eliza Wheeler lived in Triana, Alabama. According to the 1910 census, Harris was paying $30 a month for rent and owned a radio. He and Eliza were listed as being able to read and write. Each was considered a laborer on a home farm. They were members of the Saint Paul Methodist Church of Triana. It is recorded that Harris Wheeler confessed Christ as his Savior at an early age.

Harris served in the military and was a Private in Troop D in the 9th United States Cavalry. Harris Wheeler received a certificate with the United States Department of Interior's Seal acknowledging his service in the 9th United States Calvary.

Harris and Eliza moved to 3949 12th Avenue, Birmingham, Alabama, and joined the Saint Luke A.M.E. Zion Church. They would later move to 1622 8th Avenue South, Birmingham. In the 1930 census, Harris's occupation changed to 'Grocer.' 'Papa Harris' had a Mom & Pop Store in East Birmingham during the depression. He also played the piano. His 'tinkling of the ivories' inspired his niece, Brenda Thompson Taylor, to start taking piano lessons.

When I met Shelvie in 1946, his mother, Eliza, had already passed on. Harris Wheeler passed away at 88 on October 27, 1967.

No. 1032594   3—700   Increase

United States of America

BUREAU OF PENSIONS

It is hereby certified *That in conformity with the law of the United States* Harris Wheeler *who was a* Private, Troop D, 9th United States Cavalry

is entitled to a pension at the rate of Twenty-five *dollars per month, to commence* June 4, 1926 and Fifty dollars from February 9, 1927.

Given at the Department of the Interior this thirtieth *day of* June *one thousand nine hundred and* twenty-seven *and of the Independence of the United States of America the one hundred and* fifty-first

Secretary of the Interior.

Countersigned.

Commissioner of Pensions.

Former payment covering any portion of the same time to be deducted.

123

The Wheeler Family

Above is the happy family of Harris and Eliza Wheeler. Pictured from left to right are Shelvie Wheeler, Elnora White, Lina Jackson, Louise Joiner, and John Wheeler, and sitting in front is the youngest born, Mary Helen Thompson. Four of the Wheelers are missing. They are Lillian, Frances, Corine, and Shelvie's twin brother, Shelton. All were born in Triana, Alabama, except Mary Helen. By the time she came along, the Wheelers had moved to Birmingham. In Triana, farming was the major occupation for all until they moved to the big city of Birmingham. Harris Wheeler was a sharecropper who had several families working under him in Triana.

Lillian Wheeler was the firstborn. I was not able to find a photo of Lillian. Lillian was born in 1904 in Triana, Alabama. She later moved to Chicago.

Frances Wheeler Anderson was the second-born child of Harris and Eliza's family. She was born in 1906 in Triana, Alabama. Frances endured some very difficult times. She had made a decision to move to Chicago and live there with a relative as she reared her young son without the presence of her son's dad. Frances was certainly a disciplinarian. She wanted her son to be a successful adult citizen. Frances knew that her son could not follow in the ways of some of his peers, who appeared to not care about their future. She wanted him to be independent and prosperous. One day during the course of her disciplining him, he became rebellious. At the age of 13, he walked out of the house upset with his mom --- and never returned. What a tragic story. Francis carried quite a burden for most of her remaining days.

Francis moved to Tuscaloosa, Alabama, and lived there for many years. In the end, a ray of sunshine did brighten her days. Mary Helen and her daughter, Brenda, would travel from California to visit her. My daughter, Erika, would take an interest in Francis. Erika realized that Francis had a beautiful spirit and would make trips from Columbia, South Carolina, to visit her, who resided in a special rehabilitation facility. During one visit, Erika expressed her love by making a nice poster for Francis. Erika and my son, Pauron, flew to Birmingham for her 'Home Going Celebration.' Erika sang a special song during the service,

AUNT FRANCIS
AND
HER NIECE, ERIKA
I LOVE YOU-AUNTIE

and Pauron accompanied her on the piano. The service was held at the facility. One of the nurses commented after the service and said, "This was the best Home Going Service that we have had at this place."!

Lina Parthenia Wheeler was born on June 23, 1907, in Triana (Madison County), Alabama. She was the third child born and was given the middle name 'Parthenia' in honor of her dad's mother, whose name was 'Parthenia.'

Lina attended grade school in Triana and studied nursing at Tuskegee Institute. This was the school where my senior class in Pendleton, South Carolina, visited. Of course, this trip took place many years later.

In 1929, Lina married Samuel Adams Jackson, who was a foreman in the steel mill and an entrepreneur. I recall my visits to Cousin Lina's home and Sam(as we called him).

He had a barber shop and a candy store. I believe their car garage was converted into a barbershop/store. It was right across from Lina's church. Kids would love to come into his barbershop and buy candy. Sam would cut hair, and Lina would sell the candy. My kids would be amongst those asking for candy. Lina had two daughters, Aurelia Jackson Copeland and Sami Jackson Poole.

Lina, affectionately known as "Dear," was an active member of St. Luke A.M.E Church for almost 80 years. She served in several church leadership roles, including president of the Missionary Board and secretary of the choir. Her favorite song was "May The Works I've Done Speak For Me." Of course, this song was sung at her 'Home Going Celebration.' Attending St. Luke was one of her favorite things to do, as well as reading, tending to plants, and flowers, listening to music, and cheering for the Atlanta Braves baseball team. She enjoyed fellowship with her fellow church members and a loving circle of friends and family whom she loved to entertain.

Samuel passed away in 1972. Lina would live 102 years. She passed away on November 16, 2009. Lina would operate her husband's store, then known as "The Shop," for nearly 20 years after the passing of Sam. Lina's daughters preceded her in leaving this life. Sami, the youngest daughter, passed away in 1991. Aurelia passed away at the turn of the century in 2000.

John Melvin Wheeler was the fourth child born on February 1, 1909, in Triana, Alabama. Later moved to Birmingham. John completed two years of high school. He worked for the Stockham Pipe and Fitting Company.

John was a member of 45th Street Missionary Baptist Church. John married Mary Carter on May 11, 1930, in Jefferson County, Alabama, at age 21. Mary Carter was born in 1912, and she was age 18 when they married. As best as I can remember, John loved the outdoors and enjoyed living in a rural or country setting. John and his wife, Mary, were excellent hosts and enjoyed being in the company of their friends and relatives. When you entered their home, you would see one of John's striking collections; a large bear spread out on his living room floor. It was the head, paws, and fur of an actual bear that he had hunted and captured. One of my sons would sit in their living room and just stare at that creature. I must admit it was a site to see.

John registered for his World War II draft card on October 16, 1940, at age 31. He was 5'9" and 158 pounds, according to his draft card.

127

John and Mary Wheeler had two daughters, the late Barbara Wheeler and Mable J. Worthy. They also had a son, Everett Wheeler, who lives in Huntsville with his wife, Jamesetta. They have two sons, Edderrick and Melvin. Both live in Huntsville.

John passed on at 82 on September 4, 1991.

Elnora Wheeler White was the fifth child born on September 22, 1912. She was a graduate of Alabama A & M University. She married Robert F. White, who was born in 1911 in Alabama. Elnora and Robert were married in 1943. They moved to Louisville, Kentucky, and from their union was born Larry Fulton White, their only child. Robert established a well-recognized and prominent printing business named "White Printing Company, LLC." Elnora was a Special Education teacher. She retired from the Louisville Public School System. She was a member of St. Augustine Catholic Church and Delta Sigma Theta Sorority. My daughter, Erika, was fascinated with her Aunt and Uncle and their printing business that she visited them a number of times and would always return home with some exciting stories.

Robert passed away on April 24, 1997, and Elnora was 85 when she passed away on July 30, 2003. Both are entombed in the Evergreen Mausoleum in Kentucky.

Shelvie Wheeler, Sr. was the sixth or seventh child born. The uncertainty exists because Shelvie had a twin brother, Shelton, who died as an infant. I am not sure who arrived first. Shelvie was born on June 23, 1913. We were married in Kentucky on August 30, 1948. Elnora and Robert sponsored a wonderful wedding celebration for us. Shelvie served his country honorably for twenty-one years and retired in 1963 from the United States Army at Fort Jackson Army Base in Columbia, South Carolina. After his retirement, he opened and operated 'Wheeler's Community Grocery Store on Price Avenue in Columbia and devoted twenty-five years to his customers, especially the children. He was affectionately known as "Sarge" by his family and friends.

His gift of communication and leadership was utilized to bring about positive changes in the community. Oftentimes, Shelvie held life skill sessions with children in his store. He was witty, a great debater, a comedian, and a wonderful educator. He loved life and people. No one was ever a stranger to him.

Shelvie was a very patient man who was honest and forthright. On many occasions, he publicly expressed his views on governmental and educational issues.

O, how fortunate was I to have him for 54 years!

Shelton Wheeler was born the sixth or seventh child on June 23, 1913. He was Shelvie's twin brother. I am not sure which one arrived first.

It has been said that Shelton had some serious medical issues at birth and was here for a very short while.

Corine Wheeler was the eighth child born in 1915 in Triana, Alabama.

I do not have a photo or any more information about Corine.

Louise Wheeler Joiner was the ninth child born on July 26, 1919. Louise graduated from Parker High School in 1937. She later received a Bachelor's degree from Miles College in Fairfield, Alabama. After teaching school in Birmingham, Louise moved to Chicago and taught school and later took business courses that led to a job with the Internal Revenue Service as a clerical assistant, where she worked for many years. Louise also worked at Marshall Fields Department Store as an accountant and bookkeeper. While in Chicago, she met and married Charles Reaves. Louise and Charles enjoyed many years of marriage. Charles passed away, and later Louise met Edward Joiner, and the two decided to marry. They would move to Huntsville, Alabama, where Louise would work for the City of Huntsville School system and the housing authority. After retiring, Louise enjoyed traveling and spending time with her loved ones and friends. She was a favorite among her nieces and nephews.

Mary Helen Thompson was the youngest and the tenth child born on September 19, 1923, in Birmingham, Alabama, to Harris and Eliza Wheeler. She graduated from Parker High School and continued on to get her Bachelor's Degree at Tuskegee Institute. Mary Helen married Jonathan H. Thompson on February 24, 1947. Jonathan was affectionately called "Joe." Joe and Mary Helen attended the same high school and graduated the same year. They attended the same church. They also were both born in the same year. Joe graduated from Miles College. Joe had military service in the U.S. Army. Mary Helen was a high school teacher who taught English but was gifted in many other areas of discipline. Mary Helen was active in the school's drama program and assisted with plays and singing. I guess this was one of the reasons her daughter, Brenda, became an excellent musician and a nurse. Mary Helen also enjoyed sewing and was known as a gifted seamstress.

Shelvie and I enjoyed visiting Mary Helen and Joe Thompson, along with Shelvie's other relatives in Alabama. It was a sad day when Mary Helen and her family decided to move to California in 1963 but understandably so. There were a lot of bombings going on in Birmingham at the time when George Wallace was governor. As a postal clerk and letter carrier, Joe got a great opportunity in California, and he seized that moment and moved his family there. That move would later become beneficial for my sons, who got an opportunity to march in the Rose Bowl Parade on January 1, 1966, in California. While the Columbia High Band from Columbia, South Carolina, was making arrangements for the seven-day train ride to Pasadena and for their overnight stay. Shelvie and I were able to make arrangements for our three sons to stay with the Thompson Family, and they had a wonderful time. Shelvie Jr. played the trombone. Harris played the trumpet, and Pauron played the saxophone.

Mary Helen and Joe continued to enjoy their new home in California. Both would eventually retire from their professions. They had a beautiful daughter, Brenda, to enjoy, their handsome son, Orestes, and their 'full of life' grandkids, Christopher and Allison.

Jonathan H. Thompson passed away on January 20, 1991, and Mary Helen passed away in 2017.

Pauline's Parents And The Vance Family

To the right is my mother; just seeing and knowing the job her hands performed is a joy indeed. She transitioned to glory at age 95 in Pendleton, South Carolina. Death is a great enemy. This dreadful monster tackles and strangles our thoughts, stuns our actions, and stimulates tears. Of course, the knowledge of our Creator's provision for dying should forever be an affront in our minds. Then, those crushing moments become smoothed, and joy surges beyond death and centers on those peaceful days of preparation for the inevitable. I pause to reflect and consider her life, work, and achievement, seeking to gain inspiration and courage to meet the trials and tribulations of mortal existence. As a leader in the community, she built a temple of honor, virtue, and unselfish devotion to duty. The simplicity and sweetness of her character have endeared

133

her to us. A rare friendliness and charm of personality deprive us now. We speak only of her in a superlative manner. Her grace and wisdom are equal only to her courageous determination, which she strove for a better life for us. She would always say to shun gossip. Words have power; some illustrate, some aggravating, some detonate, but few fall on listing ears and fail to communicate. There are some words that savor and turn over in our minds because they feed, refresh and uplift us. Words can knock you unconscious and also encourage you. Sometimes you are afraid to try new things because you are afraid of failure. You won't fail as long as you keep getting up when you are knocked down.

Pauline Williamns Vance engaged in religious studies at the Fuller Norman Institute of Theology in Greenville, S.C. and be came an Evangelist

My mother, Pauline Williams Vance, was born June 30, 1894, in Pendleton, S.C., and died in 1989. Her union with my father brought into the home seven children. We were taught to care for each other. She was the glue that kept all of us smiling most of the time. They didn't have the finance to purchase cloth to make our clothes. In those days, flour and meal were purchased in sacks. The sacks were made in such a way that when empty, mother would pull a certain string, and then it would unravel. She would boil the empty sacks in a large black pot. Then she would place the chosen color of leaves gathered from the forest in the boiling water to give the sacks the color she wanted and then make our dresses. She drafted her own pattern. She would save the strings and wrap our hair at night and give us pretty braids the next morning for school. We were proud of her knowledge and imagination. She would see a dress in Hunters Store

134

In this pot food was cooked on top of the stove

that we liked, and when she could find enough papers, she knew how to draft the pattern. In those days, washing machines had not been invented. So the White race had their dirty clothes washed and ironed by our race (of course, we thought they were rich, but they were not.) It was our way of earning little money. Our parents taught us all they knew. They attended a one-room schoolhouse, which was open three months out of a year. During planting and harvest seasons, we were in their fields, hoeing and gathering their crops. The one-room schoolhouse was on the same property as Kings Chapel Church in Pendleton, S.C., right beside our grandmother's house. I understand the teacher was paid $10. 00 per month, and no degree was required, just since that person could read and write. We were a family grieving when our mother bade us goodbye. Oh! She was the essence of compassion and duty. She was a standard bearer for the downtrodden. Also, a brand of magic. Thanks for the way you brightened our lives. We despaired at our loss, but the message you gave us through the years afforded us the strength to move forward. Your energy, you could barely contain. I hope through your spiritual and emotional knowledge for the years ahead; we will give thanks for a woman that I am so proud to call my mother. Your unique beauty will never be extinguished from our minds.

A pan to fry food in

She died on February 20, 1989. To mom and dad, seven children were born: Elouise, Lorraine, Pauline, Thomas Jr., Fredda, Hattie, and Charles. At this date, only two of us are still living, Charles and myself. Mother was busy all the time. Farmers only had money in the fall of the year as that was the time to pick cotton and carry it to the mill to be baled and sold. It was

135

interesting watching how syrup and molasses were made. The mule was harnessed and connected to a long pole extending to a heated pot. He was trained to go round and round to squeeze the heated juice out of their cane. Then the juice would be boiled down to your desired thickness depending on whether you wanted syrup or molasses. Mother was an expert when it came to cooking. Her third-grade education was amazing. She said in her day, they were only in school about three months a year. School for blacks was closed the rest of the year so they could work on the farm. Most of the farmers were sharecroppers. We were blessed as our parents owned their farm.

Mother would say: I don't want your children left behind. The world is a battle for control between the wise and the unwise. I want you to be wise. You can only spend your life once. The best way is with vision and view. She would say those who are masquerading, trying to find a quick fix, only find trouble down the road and are not for you to admire. She would say just put a flame in your heart and do your best daily, and you would be bound for success. She really laid the foundation for our happiness.

A mold to give the butter a beautiful shape after its taken out of the churn

Mother said her ancestors were probably stolen while playing in the sand in Africa, placed on a ship, and sent to America. They crossed the sea carrying in their body the seed for the free. They worked hard in the fields, causing the cotton and the corn to yield. For years in the deep south put a prayer in their mouth, a dream like steel in their soul, and made them forget they were poor. Sometime the valley was filled with tears, but they kept on trudging through the lonely years. Sometimes the fields were as hot as the sun, but they kept on till their work was done. They are the seeds that cause you to be free.

In the 1930s, insurance companies would send out agents, who would go from door to door to try to enroll customers. Our house was a short distance from the main road. A sweet potato area was a few feet from the yard. They would dig up potatoes, brush off some of the dirt and eat away. They would address the adults as uncle and aunt instead of Mr. or Mrs. Wonder; why? They were not related because these were white people. I guess they didn't know the difference. They smile (just trying to get more customers).

Evangelist Vance was a wonderful mother. After all of her children were grown, she engaged in religious studies at the Fuller Norman Institute of Theology in Greenville, S.C. Among the many services rendered to her church were being the teacher of Sunday School class, Vice President of Women's Missionary Society, and member of the Ladies Aid Society. She was with us for 95 years.

My father, Mr. Thomas Vance, was born in Pendleton, South Carolina February 22, 1885, and died on December 21, 1973. My dad had an orchard with plenty of apples, pears, plums, peaches, and grapes. In the fall season, there were persimmons and locus trees, of which dad knew how to make beer. He also made wine from grapes. I wish now that I had acquired some of his skills. He had only a third-grade education, but he was very smart and loaded with plenty of common sense.

We had turkeys, guineas, chickens, and at least two acres of fruit trees. . We called dad the jack of all trades. He had a shoe lass, and when the sole of our

shoes wore out, he would buy the leather and put on a new sole on the shoes, and his work looked neat too. We had better not look like we disagreed with his discipline. He knew how to punish you with his eyes. That look was all you needed. I marveled at his wisdom.

I was the 3rd child. Sometime I imagine I found myself being bounced around on your knees. I can almost hear the steady rhythm of your feet and the laughter as you propelled me up and down. Your heart must have been bubbling with joy as I was your little clown. I can almost feel the crispness in the air as I trudged beside you and the plow as I held on to the lines and guided that mule as best I knew how. We tilled the soil on our farm, producing all our grain, corn, cotton, cane, and vegetable. We never agonized over playing games as children do now. There was no time for such. There were no newspapers, T.V., or radio in our home, but I hoped we could create a show of our own. Sorry you are not around. However, you provided me with the tools by allowing me to stay in school. Oh, you equipped us for life. We would rise before dawn to visit the traps you made for possums, rabbits, or whatever you would catch. I will always remember how to curry the mules with that iron comb and to have them groomed before going to school. You were a master trainer when it came to rearing your children. I was supposed to have been a boy. Sorry, nature pulled an April fool on you. Of course, you made a boy out of me anyway. I treaded along at the barn daily. You taught me how to soothe a bee sting---just wipe some of your tobacco juice on the sting. My! My! How you could spit that stuff. I will never forget the day I was supposed to purchase you a plug of tobacco after school, and I never thought about it again until I looked up and saw you and the mule. You whipped me unmercifully.

The above is a churn, which is a container where butter is made from cream by shaking or beating the content

I can almost feel the sting from the rope that you used. I am not so forgetful anymore (grin). You taught me many things that I can be proud of, but most of all, you taught us how to love each other. We learned how to be proud of our family name and in no way be disrespectful. You never spared the rod. The lessons I learned along the way are with me daily. You criticized and found fault with most of the things we did, but that was your way of making us better people. Now I have a profound understanding of your ideas, and it has allowed me to see past your faults, and I am grateful for that. I lived to see you become worn and grey. Too many periods of stress you encountered along the way. The sunset of life settled around you, and your spirit said you were through. I have not seen your face since 1973. The angels seized you. Were you eager to leave

us? It is strange, I don't remember any-thing you bought me, but I do remember the unconditional love that is far more pre-cious than gold. I remember your laugh-ter, your conversation, your presence, and

your personality glows as if it was a portrait hanging on the wall. Today I marvel at your wisdom, your guidance, and your caring. You stand mighty tall. You must have known those were the only gifts you could give me that would last a lifetime. Your gifts are embedded in my heart forever. Thank you, dad.

The Vance Family Reunion on June 29, 1979, was our first family reunion. What a momentous occasion, dreaming of our dear ancestors. A dream nourished by the blood of our ancestors of Pendleton, South Carolina. Nurtured by the sadness of their struggle, tested by the flame of oppression, tempered by means of inhumanity, sustained by survival and victories, and crippled by undying dreams brings us here. We have to keep on trying over and over again to make their dreams come true. Let us make ourselves a committee of one and feed on ideas that will stimulate a greater reunion next time. To our parents and all of us, we say no one is as sweet as you; that is why you are getting this appreciation from your children, grands, great grands, and great, great grands too. Before we were old enough to go to school, you had already taught us the golden rule. Mother Martha worked hard and proved to be a loving wife. She tried to educate her children so they could have a better life. During her golden years, she did not slow down; she kept trusting and working for a crown. She believed in going to church and helping the neighbors too. Now, this is the age of Afro-American pride. They made it possible for us to have access to a sweeter life. We thank them with the totality of our being: from the balcony of our enchanted minds, through the middle concourse of our searching hearts, to the wine cellar of our deep souls –we thank you. We must continue to throw light on their struggle and crystallize them into reality. The real purpose of our life is to renew one's spirit and inner soul with Christ's Spirit. Remembering always that we are God's creation in His universe. Made in His image, we must live with the same love that he has shown us. The union of Martha Burt and Augustus Thomas Vance produced eight children: Manuel, Stewart, Freda, Anna, Amelia, Thomas, Sidney, Charlie, and Conyers. This is a picture of grandfather Augustus' dining room after it was renovated. A few interior walls were removed and replaced with columns, and a patio, office, and kitchen were added. The home's interior was open briefly for tours. It had a plaque high on a pole as the first African American historical marker in the upstate, approved by the Upstate Department of Archives and History.

The Vance Family

From left to right: Pauline Vance Wheeler, Lorraine Vance McCaskill, Frieda Mae Vance Saunders, Hattie Vance Smith, and in the back towering over his sisters is Charles Andrew Vance, Sr. Missing are Eloise Vance Battle and Thomas Vance, Jr.

King's Chapel & Portrait of The Vance Family in 1909. This was the bulletin cover for our 1982 family reunion.

Thomas and Pauline Vance Family

Eloise Vance Battle was the 1st child of Thomas and Pauline Williams Vance. She was born on December 27, 1915. At an early age, Eloise became a member of Kings Chapel A.M.E. Church. She graduated from Anderson County Training School, and she continued to further her education at Seneca Junior College, where she received her associate degree.

Eloise moved to New York and pursued a career in nursing. She attended the Metropolitan School of Infant Care. Eloise also attended the Medical Aid Training School in New York. It was in New York where she met and married James Battle of Bronx, New York. During her many years of residency in New York, she became a member of Mt. Zion Methodist Church. There she became the President of the Courtesy Board and Secretary of the Trustee Board. Eloise had many rewarding years of service as a nurse working with geriatrics and working in convalescent care for homes and hospitals in Bronx, New York. Eloise was not only dedicated to nursing, but she was also an elegant seamstress and designer.

After forty-five years of living in New York, Eloise returned home to Pendleton, South Carolina, to care for her mother. She reunited with Kings Chapel and became active with the Senior Choir, Sunday School, and Women's Missionary Society.

Lorraine Vance McCaskill was the 2nd child born on July 7, 1919. She attended Anderson County Training School and graduated at age 17. Home Economics was one of her areas of study. Lorraine went to Seneca Junior College in Seneca, South Carolina. She studied to become a teacher. Lorraine relocated to Brooklyn, New York, desiring to find work that would help her to continue her education. She found a position at Brookdale Hospital in the diet department and worked there for 15 years. Lorraine married Reverend Paul Davis in 1945. To that union, one son was born and named after his father, Paul Davis. Reverend Paul Davis died in November of 1948. Lorraine remarried on June 1, 1961, to Curvan McCaskill. Curvan died in 1981 from wounds in an automobile accident. Lorraine retired in 1987 as an inspector for the Racing Association. In March 2001, she moved to Anderson, South Carolina, only 14 miles from her hometown, Pendleton. Lorraine enjoyed living for Christ. She credits her Mother for rearing Christian children. Also, her former late husband was very strong spiritually and liked to sing, and was an assistant pastor of AME Zion Church. Lorraine was active with senior citizens and participated in an exercise class. She enjoyed cooking. Lorraine greatly appreciated her wonderful parents because they reared her in the way she should go.

I, Pauline Vance Wheeler, was the 3rd child born on August 15, 1922. I and all of my brothers and sisters were members of King's Chapel A.M.E Church. I continued that tradition with my four boys and one girl. We all, including Shelvie, were members of Bethel A.M.E. Church, located in the heart of downtown Columbia, South Carolina. I have, unfortunately, seen three of my children pass on from this life ahead of me. Of course, at 99, I can look forward to seeing them soon. This is a wonderful blessed hope that Christians can embrace. I now have two remaining sons. They have been so kind and dependable and continually by my side, helping me to finish my course gracefully. It is good to see the fruits from all of my labor, including the whippings I gave them. They are now grown-up angels being a great help to their mom.

Harris, the older of the two remaining sons, says, "I still fear getting another whipping from you, mom." I say, "As well you should, I am still your mother, and yes, I still have a switch close by." My other son, Pauron, says, That is not a switch, mom. That is an extension cord!" My two sons reminisce and laugh at those days when I would whip them. And yes, with an extension cord, it has certainly achieved the desired results. Both of my sons are doing well and can look back and laugh at those days.

Now let me share about my grand and great-grandchildren. My son, Pauron, and Mirian Turner have given me a grandson, Steven Turner. Pauron and his wife, April Burden Wheeler, have given me a granddaughter, Sierra Deborah Wheeler. My son, Harris, and his wife, Rhetta Sumter Wheeler, have given me two grandchildren. They are Troy Jermaine Wheeler and Dionne La Shawn Wheeler Henderson. Troy and his wife from Sierra Leone, Musu Francis Wheeler, have given me a great-granddaughter, Mende Michelle

Wheeler. Dionne and her husband, Brian Henderson, have given me two great-grandchildren: Kingston Wheeler and Nia Rose Wheeler.

Thomas Vance, Jr. was the 4th child born on May 6, 1924. Thomas attended Anderson County Training School. He was a member of King's Chapel A.M.E Church. Thomas was a wonderful brother. He was so good at helping around the house. I remember one unfortunate decision that my dad made regarding Thomas that would hurt Thomas for a long time. This is the story.

My dad had a fairly large farm with orchards, corn, chickens, and pigs, and that's just to name a few. One day while Thomas was assisting his dad, who was so proud of his son Thomas, dad offered Thomas the choice of one of his pigs that would become his own. Thomas was so thrilled to have a pig of his own. He looked over all the pigs and chose one. After he pointed to the one he wanted, dad said, "OK, Thomas, that will be your pig." Thomas took great care of his pig. Everyone could tell that Thomas was happy about owning a pig. One day, dad decided to have a pig sale. The news spread that dad was selling his pigs. There was a gentleman that came out to buy a pig from dad. Dad took the man to see his pigs and told him to pick out the one that he wanted. The customer looked them over and picked out a pig to buy. Unfortunately, he had chosen Thomas' pig. Instead of dad apologizing to his customer, letting him know that the pig he had chosen belonged to his son, dad was silent. Dad sold him his son's pig. O, how sad was Thomas for a long time when he found out that dad had sold his pig. To make matters worst, Thomas did not get one dime from the sale of his pig. Thomas tried to reason with dad but to no avail. This weighed on Thomas for a long time. It certainly affected his relationship with his dad.

Thomas went on to serve his country in the military. Thomas had an untimely death at age 54. He passed away on May 21, 1978. He departed this life leaving behind a daughter named Sharon R. Vance.

Frieda Mae Vance Saunders was the 5th child born on July 14th, 1927, in Pendleton, South Carolina, to Thomas and Evangelist Pauline Vance. Frieda attended Anderson County Training School. She was a member of King's Chapel A.M.E. Church.

In 1948, Frieda moved to New York City and worked as a nurse practitioner for several years. It was in New York where she met Lloyd D. Saunders. Frieda married in 1959, and from this union came five daughters. Frieda then took on the role of a homemaker to pursue the full-time job of parenting her daughters.

Several years later, Frieda would return to the workforce. This time she worked for a company called Building Maintenance. She worked for over ten years and then retired.

The hobbies that Frieda enjoyed were indoor gardening, sewing, and solving crossword puzzles. Frieda was a member of St. Matthew's Baptist Church for over forty years, where she served as Deaconess.

Lloyd and Frieda Saunders's daughters are Wilma Vance Capers, Sylvania Saunders, Patricia Saunders, Lenora Saunders-McInnis, and Valerie Saunders. Her grandchildren are Lawrence Vance, Wilhelma Vance, Shameka Brown, and James Saunders.

Hattie Vance Smith was the sixth child born on May 19, 1930. I was very fortunate to have Hattie's biography written by Hattie. Here is her own account of her life.

"I grew up on a 40-acre farm as the seventh of eight sisters and brothers. Boredom was not in the distance of our vocabulary. My parents were financially poor and had limited educational skills. They had a striving mentality and cultural endeavor that separated them from people who thought of themselves as superior. They believed in educating the whole child and did exercise that belief with us all.

I entered school at the age of five. Walked 2 ½ miles to and from school daily. One hundred days a year, rain, snow, cold, hot, sick, or well. The school bus passed us every day, but we were not allowed to ride. We did not whisper thoughts about caring to ride. We did not voice our opinion with bus riders who opened school bus windows to throw litter at us. Labeled us with name-calling and using inappropriate language. Once I had a chance to reflect on those years, all insults were used as stepping stones to a greater evaluation of self-worth. I received my diploma at the age of fifteen from the Anderson County Training School (ACTS). Attended and received a Bachelor of Arts Degree from Allen University and Benedict College at the age of nineteen. I attended graduate school at Pennsylvania State University. I also attended South Carolina State College in Orangeburg, S.C., and Clemson University.

I thought I had many chores to complete at home. I was never denied the opportunity to participate in activities at school. I sang in the Glee Club and played basketball for four years. I participated in Sunday School and church activities.

I was joined in Holy matrimony in 1955. To that union, two boys were born. They have lived successful lives. Both have married, and I have the bragging rights of sharing and caring for three grandchildren.

I chose to teach as a vocation. I taught in public school at Westminster High School, W.M. Anderson Elementary School in Kingstree, Pendleton Elementary, and Riverside School in Pendleton, S.C. After 33 years of dedicated service in the public school system, I retired in 1982. I have been retired for 21 years and have found it to be very rewarding to meet and talk with former students. Most of them are married and enjoying family life and vocations that they chose. They have expressed to me their thanks for the strict guidance and motivation that help them to build a foundation for positive thinking and goal, reaching for a happy life. It is my greatest hope that these parents, by their daily actions, will pass on to their children a legacy of learning with rewarding consequences.

Hattie's great source of joy were her children and her grand-children. She worked cheerfully and tirelessly in assisting in their education. Her firstborn of two sons was Terence Hassan. Terence and his wife, Pamela, have two children: Anisah Hassan and Bakari Hassan. Hattie's second son is Fitzgerald Vance Smith. Fitzgerald and his wife, Natashya, have three children: Kira Smith, Nicole Smith and Thomas Smith. Hattie provided after school teaching to all five of her grands. After school, she served them a hot meal and immediately following, they were expected to "get their lessons". She always felt that children could not learn if they were hungry.

The following song was arranged especially for Aunt Hattie and sung to her on her community-wide birthday celebration, May 19, 2018. This occasion was a most deserving tribute to many years of selflessly giving of herself to caring for her loved ones.

Here is my brother, Charles Vance, own accounts.

"Doing a history of my life's journey through the years is quite a challenge for me. I am the 7th child born to Mr. and Mrs. Thomas Vance on June 20, 1937, says my mother, although my birth certificate reads the 25th of June 1937.

I was born in the house of my parents' humble farmland of many acreages embodying farm equipment, livestock, orchards, wetlands, and new ground that was cultivated into a variety of crops. I vividly remember the scuppernong grapes vines, the blueberry, strawberry patches, and vegetable gardens that were tended and usually in view of the house.

I cherish my membership in the church that was built on the highest point of elevation in the town of Pendleton, established and incorporated by Vance and other founding fathers, whose address is 135 Vance Street, Pendleton, S.C. 29670. I attended King Chapel African Methodist Episcopal Church all of my formative years, serving as a member of our Junior Choir, a youth Usher as well as an active member of The A.C.E.L. (African Christian Endeavor League). My mother, Mrs. Pauline Vance, served many years as a missionary, trustee, and minister of the gospel at Kings Chapel A.M.E. Church.

The school for Black Americans was about six miles from our farmland. There were no school buses for us in 1942. I was taken to our school one cold day by my sisters because I should not be left at home alone. This was my first day at school. Ms. McAdams saw me in the assembly area that morning and asked what my name and age were. I replied Five and Charles. She then asked me if I would like to come to stay for a day with her in her first-grade class, instructing me that I must be quiet and orderly. I gladly accepted as this was my first day in a classroom at A.C.T.S. (Anderson County Training

School) in Pendleton, South Carolina. There were teachers that left a lasting impression on me growing into adulthood. To name a very few, Mrs. S. McAdams, Mrs. Mamie Crawford, my 4th-grade teacher, a very stern and fair diction educator, Mrs. Hodges, Mrs. Helen McDowell, and Mr. Rufus Thompson, an educator, and principal. My major was shop and wood crafting. I was on the football team along with Charlie Carter, my mentor. Oh! I must tell this when we played other high school football teams: the opposing teams were frightened of us after being told that our (A.C.T.S.) team was a ruthless and mean reform school team. I attended here from first grade through graduation in 1955, graduating a year early. This was the year that A.C.T.S. was replaced with a new school complex named "Riverside."

After graduating, I enlisted in the U S Air Force. I was assigned to Shilling Air Force Base, The Strategic Air Command, and the 802 Air Division for B47 Bomber Aircraft Wing located in Salina, Kansas. I was a support crew member and Egress Supervisor. After serving six years, I was honorably discharged in 1962. During my tenure in the military, I subscribed to The New York Civil Service Centennial Newspaper, and at every opportunity, I applied for any exam that was of my interest. Upon each of my military leaves, I took the New York Civil Service Test to prepare for a profession as a civilian. The tests I took and passed were: Post Office Clerk, Port Authority Police, Transit Subway Motorman, Court Correction, and Police. I attended John J. College of Criminal Justice on West 59th Street, where I took electives to become a liaison officer assigned to the Supreme Court of Brooklyn, N.Y. On the 26th of August 1967, I purchased a two-family house in Canarsie on 103 Street and Avenue "J" in Brooklyn for my family, my wife Soja, and two sons, Charles and Charlton. I retired from my Civil Service employment in June of 1985. I traveled to the East in 1972 and became a Carthaginian Mason in Lodge #47 of Brooklyn. After retiring, I became a travel agent for Akin Tours on Flatbush Ave in Brooklyn. After a year in the travel industry, I became a tour guide for the same agency and remained in that employment until 1990. I transferred to Twin Travel Agency in Starrett City, Canarsie,

Brooklyn. There, I became the assistant manager. This was the community where I had purchased a house years earlier after I left the military. I became an Amateur Citizen Band operator by a radio transmitter and receiver and communicating to certification.

Also, I acquired a Green Belt in Korean Karate as a security blanket to aid in street protection. Upon retiring from the Twin Pines Travel desk, I sold my house on 103rd street and moved to Rockville Centre on Long Island, New York, where I met my now deceased wife Eugenia O'Brien of almost 15 years. We were avid social dancers known as Ebony and Ivory of ballroom circles. Her passing was a very difficult time in my life. In1999, Eugenia and I purchased a house in Hershey' Mill Estates in Westchester, Pennsylvania. We were in Westchester in summer and in winter in our condo at The Marriott Resort in Florida. Upon Eugenia's passing in 2015, I purchased a condo in Leisure World in Silver Spring just outside of Washington, D.C., and I now commute by Amtrak Auto train from Lorton, Virginia, to Stanford, Florida. Just as my luck will have it, I met a darling, gorgeous lady at our automobile dealership in Silver Spring, Maryland, who is the love of my life. A darling who answers to "Sallie Letterlough" each time I speak her name, she is precious.

My Sister Pauline asked me to write this life's journey of myself; anyone else would very likely have to put my words in print themselves for this to become my life' journey record.

When my sister Pauline asked me to put this journey in writing, I said to her smilingly, "what's the rush? You're only 98. We've got plenty of time yet. (smile)"

Sincerely Yours,
Brother Charles

Above is a picture of our last reunion that took place on July 13, 2019, in Richmond, Virginia.

The organizational leadership was provided by Anisah Hassan, daughter of Terence and Pamela Hassan, and she was assisted by Dionne Henderson. During the program part of this family reunion, the opening welcome was given to Little Miss Mende Wheeler, daughter of Troy and Musu Wheeler. Dionne continued with the 'Introduction.' The blessing of the food was given by Dionne's dad, Harris Wheeler. Everyone participated in the "Reflections" segment of the meeting then Harris spoke to us on the theme, "Continuing in Togetherness." His message included planning for the next reunion. The closing prayer for the event was given by April Wheeler.

Thanks to the initiative of Anisah Hassan and Dionne Henderson, The Vance Family continues with family meetings. During the Covid Virus, we would have Zoom meetings. What a new way of communicating! It was rather an enjoyable experience.

Acknowledgments

I desire to take the time to express a word of gratitude and thanks to family, friends, and ministries who helped me to get across the finish line in completing this memoir. The Vance Family, The Wheeler Family, and The Baldwin Family have been a source of inspiration and encouragement.

My two sons and my late daughter, Erika, stayed with me about writing my story. I did make some small attempts but was not able to be consistent. Living with my daughter during her bout with ALS was upsetting to watch. In early November 2018, when Erika passed away, my son, Pauron, and his family moved in to assist me. I went through a period of mental and physical restoration. Around the year 2020, I began watching TBN (Trinity Broadcasting Network). TBN broadcasts a number of ministries. It was also around this time on Sundays that my other son, Harris, would access on my computer, "From The Heart Ministries," in Maryland. After a while, I started to look forward to listening to Joyce Myers, John Cherry (Father & Son), and Joel Osteen. It was around the Fall of 2020 that I could see myself progressing mentally and physically. During this time, I began to write my story with consistency. I thought that I would include the pictures of these three ministries as a gesture of appreciation for their faith-filled messages.

Joyce Meyer Ministries   From The Heart Ministries   Joel Osteen Ministries
Maryland
Dave & Joyce Meyer   John & LaWanda Cherry, II   Joel & Victoria Osteen

My son, who has been assisting me with my writing, had to go into surgery in early January 2022. I was really nearing the completion of my book. Pauron told me that his Surgeon informed him that the procedure was a common one. Perhaps, for two days at the most, he would be in the hospital. Unfortunately, the procedure left him paralyzed in his left arm and leg. He was to remain in the hospital for two weeks. The second surgery was successful, and he had started to regain the use of his left arm and leg. He spent four weeks at The Sheltering Arms Institute, a place that he says is one of the best on the East Coast. While Pauron says that he can't begin to name all those whom the Lord used to help in his recovery, he does want to acknowledge a local business and three ministries in the Richmond and Quinton area of Virginia. They provided prayers for my son.

Doug Wurz
&
The Richmond Piano Family

Save America Ministries	Providence UMC	From The Heart Ministries
Richmond, Virginia	Quinton, Virginia	Richmond, Virginia
Chuck & Kathie Crismier	Bill & Jenny John	James & Tresa Ransom

Brenda Thompson Taylor

I would like to acknowledge my niece, Brenda Taylor, who was able to give me information that I did not have about the Wheeler Family and provided some editing. Brenda lives in California and is enjoying her retirement as a nurse.

Thanks To Everett L. Wheeler

I would like to acknowledge my cousin, Everett Wheeler, the Wheeler Family's historian. Everett has done a lot of research on the Wheeler Family, and I appreciate his contribution.

Thanks To The Baldwin Family

Jewell Baldwin Cousin Constance (Connie) Morris Cynthia Johnson Tilly Carolyn Baldwin Tucker

This family has been a year-round source of love and inspiration. I appreciate all of your correspondence.

Thanks To Dianne Jordan & Phyllis Ward

Pauron left for surgery on January 11th and returned home on February 25th. He had scheduled his vacation time during his surgery but only had two weeks of vacation time.

It wasn't too long before Pauron had no source of revenue, but my son loved the Lord and was not worried at all. Soon he got a call from a member of the Providence Church Family. Two dear sisters in the Lord decided to set up a "Give Send Go" account for him. Over three thousand dollars was raised. That money, along with contributions, was mailed to him and the money given to his wife and daughter when they attended church was enough to sustain him through the Spring. As a tribute to their initiative, the following is a picture of Dianne and Phyllis, who set up the account and website for Pauron.

Dianne Jordan   Phyllis Ward

Thanks To Joan VanDervort

Joan was so helpful in getting me some valuable information that greatly contributed to my completing this book.

Thanks To The Sidney Vance Family

Katrenia Vance   Sylvester Vance   Derick Vance   Ann Vance   Errol Vance

In the above picture, Katrenia's brother, Sylvester, and His wife, Ann, are no longer with us. Derick and Errol are her nephews.

Katrenia is the Vance Family historian on my dad's brother's side of the family. Her full name is Paula Katrenia Vance, Missouri. His name is Sidney Augustus Vance. Katrenia is his granddaughter. Sidney and His wife, Rebecca, had ten children. They were Walter, Bailous, Garfield, Gus, Martha, Annamelia, Katie, and Connie. Katie is Katrenia's mother. The two that are not mentioned passed away as infants. Sidney and Rebecca's family lived in Pendleton, South Carolina. According to Katrenia, Sidney was affectionately called "Papa Sidney." Prior to his leaving us, he had twenty-four

162

grandchildren and nineteen great-grandchildren. Papa Sidney's demeanor was described as easygoing with a distinctive, hearty laugh that could be heard "a mile away."

Thanks again, Katrenia, for providing the following picture of your grandfather, Sidney Augustus Vance, with his grandson, Sylvester, standing next to him.

Thanks For Professional Assistance

I would like to thank Chandler Bolt, Sofia Antonio and Coach Barbara Hartzler of Self-Publishing School, PostcardMania, Pensacola Christian College & Abeka Copyright Permissions, Stefanie Newell-Ross How To Write Your First Book, the National Personnel Records Center, the Library of Congress and ALA (American Library Association), The State Newspaper of Columbia, South Carolina, The Healing Advocates (Alan Scott Douglas and Patricia Tamowski), Wireless Education (Cece Doucette), Hal Leonard and Concord Music Publishing. I appreciate the excellent service that you have provided.

Thanks To Michelle Obama

To Pauline,
Movements for real and lasting change are sustained by the
relationships we build with one another.
Thank you for your support.   *Michelle Obama*

The movement that Michelle Obama started was "GARDENING"! It was in 2014 when Michelle got America to think about eating healthy foods. She realized that America's citizens were in trouble with our lifestyle when it came to food. Michelle even had youth come to the White House to help her with gardening. Well, gardening is what I do! Here are some pictures that I sent Michelle, and she was so kind to respond!

Spring  2014

I would not have enjoyed 54 years of marriage to Shelvie had I not learned how to forgive my husband.

LET US LOVE WITH THE LOVE OF THE LORD

&

FORGIVE AS CHRIST HAS FORGIVEN US

Made in United States
North Haven, CT
07 May 2023

36363996R00095